THE LONGEVITY
CHINESE
VEGETARIAN
COOKBOOK

Appetizing, authentic Eastern recipes made with healthy natural foods

THE LONGEVITY CHINESE VEGETARIAN COOKBOOK

Outstanding Pritikin-style recipes —
no added fat, salt, oil, sugar or MSG!

Margaret Gee and Graeme Goldin

THORSONS PUBLISHING GROUP
Wellingborough, Northamptonshire

Rochester, Vermont

First published in Australia by the Tortoiseshell Press as
The Longevity Chinese Cookbook, 1985.

This revised edition first published in Great Britain 1987.

British Library Cataloguing in Publication Data

Gee, Margaret
The longevity Chinese vegetarian cookbook:
outstanding Pritikin-style recipes, no
added fat, salt, oil, sugar or MSG. —
Rev. ed.
1. Cookery, Chinese
I. Title   II. Goldin, Graeme   III. Gee,
Margaret, Longevity Chinese cookbook
641.5'637'0951   TX724.5.C5

ISBN 0-7225-1459-X

Reproduced, printed and bound in Great Britain by
Hazell Watson & Viney Limited,
Member of the BPCC Group,
Aylesbury, Bucks

1 3 5 7 9 10 8 6 4 2

CONTENTS

Photography by Robbi Newman.

Artwork by Ken Gilroy.

Black and white photographs of China by Bruce Miller.

Preparation of food for photography by
home economist Susan Whitter.

Dinnerware supplied by Fitz and Floyd,
Kosta Boda and Villeroy and Boch.

THE LONGEVITY CHINESE VEGETARIAN COOKBOOK

The recipes contained in this book are low in fat, cholesterol and protein, with no added salt, sugar, oil or monosodium glutamate.

Overall, the recipes conform strictly to the healthy eating principles outlined in the following bestselling books:

'The Pritikin Program for Diet and Exercise'
by Nathan Pritikin with Patrick M. McGrady.

'The Pritikin Promise — 28 Days to a Longer, Healthier Life'
by Nathan Pritikin.

This book is dedicated to Kath and Allan Gee, my parents, who gave the Pritikin programme a chance, and restored their health.

It is also in memory of Nathan Pritikin, and for Ilene Pritikin with gratitude.

FOREWORD

A trip to China some years ago as part of an academic group visiting Chinese universities and hospitals enabled me to see at first hand the very low incidence of coronary artery disease in China. Indeed, the only Chinese with a heart attack we examined was about the only overweight man we saw in China. But there was a considerable amount of high blood-pressure. Margaret Gee and Graeme Goldin have made full use of the Chinese experience. They have employed dietary principles expounded by Nathan Pritikin and written a book to delight Westerners who enjoy or would like to try Chinese cooking, and who are seized with the wisdom of coronary prevention rather than treatment.

There has been a highly significant recent decline in death rates from heart attack in Australia and in North America. The mortality rates had increased for decades, but 1968 saw the beginning of a decline by about 25 per cent over the next 10 years; and this decline is still continuing. There is much debate about the reasons for these improved mortality figures. But population studies undertaken in North America and published last year indicate that at least 33 per cent of this decline is due to the reductions in fat and cholesterol intake which have occurred during this period; and that reduced smoking accounts for a further 24 per cent. If these results can be obtained across the board on a population basis, how much better might the thoughtful individual do! Prevention is within the grasp of us all.

This book is an important contribution to prevention in that the recipes described not only provide the preparation of appetizing low-fat and low-cholesterol meals, but they also pay particular attention to reducing the high salt intake associated with traditional Chinese cooking. The latter has been a drawback in the past and may well have contributed to levels of high blood-pressure in China. The authors are fully aware of this and in these recipes have focused particular attention on salt content, which has been lowered dramatically. This objection, then, has been overcome and the book is recommended for those interested in Chinese cooking and coronary prevention.

DAVID WILCKEN, MD, FRCP, FRACP
Chairman
Department of Cardiovascular Medicine
Prince Henry and Prince of Wales Hospitals
Sydney, AUSTRALIA

INTRODUCTION

'I'd rather die than eat this rabbit food.' That was my father's initial response to the Pritikin eating plan, even though he had suffered three heart attacks, and was frequently reduced to tears by angina pain. Furthermore, he was facing — with great reluctance — the prospect of open heart surgery. My 'classic Pritikin' response to his remark was: 'Well, Dad, if you would rather die than change your diet, you will!'

Five years later and after much cajoling from me, my father now swims two kilometres a day and takes no medication, and his doctors refer to his reversal of heart disease as nothing short of 'miraculous'.

The 'miracle maker' in this instance was Nathan Pritikin, founder of the Pritikin Longevity Center in Santa Monica, California. Nathan Pritikin has become a legendary figure in the health area for his curative and preventive approach to degenerative disease through a simple, natural diet and exercise programme.

In 1980 I was the Public Relations Manager for Schwartz Publishing, which first introduced the Pritikin concept to Australia by publishing *The Pritikin Program for Diet and Exercise* in hardcover.

The Publisher, Morry Schwartz, travelled to America and gained the Australian publishing rights. He thought he had a hot bestseller on his hands. Morry was right, but had no idea the book would trigger a nutritional revolution in Australia.

Morry and I met Nathan and Ilene Pritikin and instantly warmed to this delightful unpretentious couple. During the three-week publicity campaign that ensued I came to realize that Nathan Pritikin was not just another fad American dietician. I still maintain he was a genius worthy of the Nobel prize for his outstanding research into the relationship between an unhealthy diet — laden with fat, oil, sugar and salt — and degenerative diseases such as heart disease, strokes, arthritis, diabetes, cancer, obesity and many more. Just before this book was printed I received a warm letter from Ilene Pritikin expressing her support and encouragement.

During Nathan and Ilene Pritikin's visit to Australia they bought a lot of fruit, made fabulous salad sandwiches, and ate in many restaurants. They said they adored Chinese food, and I questioned them about how they avoided the fried, salty food often served. They explained they always gave the waiters precise instructions that they wanted their food cooked without oil, and with no added salt, sugar or monosodium glutamate. They emphasized that the way to ensure the meal always arrived the way they ordered was to say at the outset that if the meal wasn't prepared the way they requested, it would be sent back.

Although top Australian Pritikin-style cooks including Toni Bobbin, Julie Stafford, Marlene Pentecost and Suzanne Porter have provided imaginative Pritikin recipes, I yearned for a book that concentrated solely on my favourite food — Chinese cuisine.

The solution was to accumulate all my own oriental recipes, and adapt them to the life-saving Pritikin preparation and cooking methods. Over the years I have continually come across people who are happy with the Pritikin eating programme, but regret having to give up Chinese food.

In 1982 I travelled to China for a 600 kilometre bicycle tour of Southern China. In the rural areas in particular we feasted on delicious food with a strong emphasis on braised and steamed dishes with minimal quantities of meat, fish or chicken. However, during that four-week trip, we were served quite a lot of salty, fried food. Recently, the Chinese authorities have directed that people should cut down on fried food and eat more steamed and braised food. The Pritikin message has now reached international proportions.

The recipes have been developed with the assistance of Graeme Goldin, an Australian doctor specializing in radiology and, in his spare time, the pursuit of gourmet Chinese cooking. Graeme has enthusiastically and tirelessly created many of the superb recipes presented here. My twin sister Christine Gee has also contributed a couple of tasty recipes inspired by her many visits to China and other parts of Asia. Special thanks are also due to Barbara Goldin and Sybil Pliner for trying out some of our recipes, and for offering helpful advice and encouragement.

My parents Allan and Kath Gee and my brother Bruce have also been a continual source of love and enthusiasm.

Sincere thanks to Morry Schwartz for his invaluable advice and support.

Best wishes and good health!
MARGARET GEE

IMPORTANT NOTE

People who need to be on the Pritikin Regression diet should limit themselves to a maximum of 3 oz (85 grams) of animal protein per week and no more than three pieces of fruit per day, and completely eliminate dried fruit — as well as sticking to the limitations involved in the Pritikin Maintenance diet.

If you are on the Pritikin Maintenance diet eat only 3–3½ oz (85–100g) of animal protein per day; a maximum of 1½ lb (680g) per week.

'WHAT CAN I EAT?'

The Pritikin eating plan recommends that you use the following foods. The foods to avoid are also listed.

	Recommended	**Avoid**
Alcohol	Moderate use. Dry white wines are preferable.	
Bean Curd	Maximum amount allowed on Maintenance Diet 3 oz (100g) per day as a substitute for meat, chicken or fish.	
Butter	None.	Margarine, all fatty dairy products.
Cereals	Wholegrain flours, breads, rice spaghetti, other pastas.	Any grain products containing added fat, oil, sugar, eggs, salt and non-wholegrain products.
Cheese	Small quantities of non-fat, Ricotta-type cheeses.	Full-fat cheeses.
Eggs	Egg whites only. Maximum 7 per week.	Egg yolks, caviar.
Fats/Oils	None.	
Fish	Fresh fish, lobster, oysters, scallops or squid. Maximum amount allowed per day on the Pritikin Maintenance diet only 3 oz (85g). This would exclude having any other animal protein during that day. On the Maintenance diet only, you can have 1½ oz (50g)	

	Recommended	**Avoid**
	of prawns or crab per day, but NO OTHER animal protein during that day.	
Fruits	Fresh if possible. Use small quantities of dried fruits only rarely.	Only use canned fruits if fresh not available. Buy those canned in natural fruit juice. Don't eat fruit jams or jellies made with sugar or honey.
Juices	Fresh fruit and vegetable juices.	Processed, canned or packaged. Fruit and vegetables are best eaten whole rather than juiced.
Meat	Trim meat of all excess fat. Use only lean cuts. *Regression diet*:Eat only 3 oz (85g) per week. *Maintenance diet*: Eat only 1½ lb (680g) per week. (This allowance is for total animal protein — meat, chicken and fish consumed per week.)	Processed meats: salami, sausages, ham, bacon, offal, liver, kidneys, brains and other organ meats.
Milk	Skimmed milk only in small quanties. Low-fat yogurt.	Cream, whole fat milk, non dairy substitutes. Commercial flavoured yogurt.
Nuts/Seeds	Small quantity chestnuts.	All other nuts. Some of the recipes in this book contain small quantities of sesame seeds. Optional.
Poultry	Lean, skinned chicken.	Duck, goose, pheasant.
Salads	Unlimited. Use only non-oil, no-added-salt- or sugar-dressings.	

	Recommended	Avoid
Sauces	Fresh only, made without oil, butter, sugar, salt, or monosodium glutamate.	Commercial sauces with added oil, salt, sugar or monosodium glutamate.
Seasonings	Use as per recipes.	Monosodium glutamate, salt or sugar.
Sugar	None.	Honey, molasses, glucose, sugar, syrup substitutes.
Tea & Coffee	Tea: Herbal teas are preferable. Coffee: None.	Decaffeinated coffee.

HOW TO COOK CHINESE FOOD 'PRITIKIN-STYLE'

The great myth about Chinese cuisine is that it is healthy. Chinese gourmets expound the benefits of crunchy stir-fried vegetables. Unfortunately most conventional Chinese cooking is saturated in oil, with added salt, sugar and monosodium glutamate.

Nutritional studies have revealed that most Chinese food available commercially is in fact just as bad as the much maligned Western junk food.

However, on a more positive note, the Chinese have one of the most original and delicious cuisines in the world — savoured by millions — and with some simple changes in cooking methods 'the real thing' is possible without harmful dietary effects.

I want to stress that it is certainly possible to eat Pritikin-style food away from home if you are explicit about how you want your food prepared.

I think you will find the majority of Chinese restaurateurs are only too pleased to conform to your wishes. I regularly eat in Chinese restaurants, and enjoy a wide variety of dishes prepared for me without oil, added salt, sugar or monosodium glutamate. You'd be surprised how few visits to your favourite Chinese restaurant it takes to train the waiters in how you like your food prepared.

The ever-increasing popularity of Pritikin-style cooking is sure to inflate the demand for this type of food in all restaurants — regardless of cuisine style. In America, Pritikin-style restaurants are flourishing, and I am sure the trend is going to accelerate elsewhere.

I have travelled extensively in China, Singapore, Japan, Malaysia, Thailand, Nepal, India, the Philippines, and the Maldives, and Asian food has always been my first preference. During the last four years I have been experimenting with trying to produce authentic Chinese food sticking rigidly to the Pritikin guidelines. Although this has meant some food normally included in Chinese dishes has been deleted, my friends and family are always eager to accept an invitation to a Pritikin-style Chinese banquet at my place.

On the Pritikin Maintenance diet you can have 1½ lb (680g) of fresh fish, chicken or meat per week. On the Pritikin Regression diet your weekly allowance of animal protein is only 3 oz (85g) per week. If you choose to eat lobsters, oysters, scallops or squid on the Maintenance diet the maximum daily allowance is 3½ oz (100g). You cannot have any more animal protein on that day.

If you want to replace your entire daily allocation of fish, meat or chicken you can have 1½ oz (50g) only of prawns or crab — Pritikin Maintenance diet only.

If you are on the Pritikin Maintenance diet you can eat a maximum of 3½ oz (100g) of bean curd per day. This would be a substitute for the daily allocation of meat, fish or chicken.

No pre-prepared sauces are used from cans or jars. All sauces have been devised using fresh, natural ingredients free of sugar, oil, salt or monosodium glutamate.

Soy sauce, the mainstay of most Chinese recipes, has been substituted with low-salt soy sauce widely available in supermarkets, health food shops and Chinese stores. Soy sauce can also be diluted with water. Many of the recipes contain no soy sauce.

Egg noodles are also out. Instead, use natural wholewheat noodles made with flour and water. Chinese stores have fresh dried noodles which are also appropriate.

Because the famous soy black beans are salted I recommend only using them in small quantities. Soaking them for 15 minutes in cold water before use reduces the salt content. After soaking rinse and drain.

The number one secret to cooking Pritikin-style Chinese food is to stir fry quickly in *boiling water or stock, not oil.* You will relish the clean, delicious, natural flavour of the food; and never again hanker after that greasy taste usually associated with stir fried in oil Chinese food.

Many of the recipes are stir fried in water, par-boiled, steamed, casseroled or dry-roasted — the healthy low-fat, low-cholesterol, way to cook tantalizing Chinese food — Pritikin-style. (*A delicious recipe tip*: when stir frying in water I recommend you use vegetable stock for added flavour.)

Use your flair and imagination and include a selection of both Chinese and local produce in your cooking.

A visit to the fruit and vegetable markets is always fun, and you will enjoy familiarizing yourself with the myriad range of Chinese fruits, vegetables and herbs.

Eggs are widely used in conventional Chinese cooking. Nathan Pritikin and I agreed that the best place for egg yolks was the rubbish bin. However, egg whites swirled through soups and other dishes are acceptable.

For rice dishes use only brown rice. Once you have experimented with brown rice I'm sure you will find white rice is gluggy and tasteless — not to mention lacking the essential nutrients and fibre brown rice provides.

Sprouts are a tasty food source, and as well as being nutritious are an attractive garnish for many of the dishes presented here. Use them liberally.

Commercially prepared traditional sauces such as chilli, lemon, hoisin, plum, oyster, and sweet and sour can't be used. You will be surprised how easy it is to make a number of these Chinese sauces using *fresh*, additive-free ingredients. Fresh lemons, oranges, mangoes, plums, and lychees will have your taste buds tingling, and the sauces will be zesty and healthy.

West Lake Watercress Soup
(page 34).

Spring Rolls (page 38).

Soy Sauce Lotus Root (page 39).

Steamed Stuffed Mushrooms with Chilli (page 43).

COOKING UTENSILS

Any visit to a Chinese store is a culinary adventure.

Stacks of multi-coloured crockery seem to teeter precariously on shelves; woks abound like miniature UFOs, and majestic steamers conjure up images of exotic Chinese banquets.

For all the recipes presented here you can either make do with your current cookware, or if you want to 'do it all Chinese style', the following items are recommended.

If you are already following the Pritikin diet your non-stick cookware will generally suffice.

Chopsticks
Many people by now have outgrown eating Chinese food with spoons and forks. Bamboo or plastic chopsticks are available, and the more expensive ones are lacquered and highly decorative. The long wooden cooking chopsticks are ideal for stirring food in the wok.

Chopper
You may have seen these rather murderous-looking weapons dangling in Chinese shops. They are ideal for hatcheting vegetables into bite-size pieces. Somehow, an ordinary cook's knife doesn't have the same impact as a traditional Chinese chopper.

Chopping Board
A sturdy wooden chopping board is a must for the seemingly endless amount of chopping, slicing and cutting that needs to be done for Chinese cuisine.

Crockery
Bowls are best for devouring Chinese food, as soups are often served during the meal. Flat plates are ideal for serving other dishes, as it is easier to pluck an item of food from a flat plate than a curved dish.

Earthenware Casserole
These dishes are ideal for slow-simmered Chinese treats, but can be substituted with your regular casserole equipment. Many Chinese earthenware dishes are not only efficient cookware, but make attractive serving dishes — from oven to table.

Ladle
A sturdy soup ladle is useful for measuring out stock, and for serving soup at the table.

Strainers

These are great for extracting a juicy morsel of food from your wok or steamboat. They have bamboo handles and many of them are made from brass mesh. They can be bought in a wide variety of sizes.

Wok

This is the premier cooking utensil used in Chinese cooking. Non-stick woks are now available, and for Pritikin recipes are far better. Flat-bottomed woks are also available for electric stove hot plates. When you clean your wok, avoid using too much detergent or scraping it with an abrasive scourer. A lid to cover your wok is also a useful item.

Wok Chan

This curved spoon is used for tossing and flipping — in this case — stir water-fried food. If you are using a non-stick wok, make sure you use a compatible non-stick wok chan which won't scratch the surface.

CHINESE INGREDIENTS

Chinese food stores are exciting and well worth visiting if you want to cook authentic Chinese cuisine.

Although many ingredients are canned or preserved, oodles of fresh and dried items can be used. If you purchase commercially produced ingredients, try to find out which ones have the least amount of added oil, salt, sugar and monosodium glutamate, as these are non-Pritikin foods.

Although Chinese cooking does require some unique and exotic ingredients many food items can be bought at your local supermarket, health food shops, fruit, vegetable and Chinese food stores.

Listed below is a sample of some ingredients which will add authenticity, flavour and nutrition to your Chinese meals.

Bamboo Shoots
Buy fresh or use only those packed in water. If using canned variety soak in cold water for 10 minutes to help remove excess salt.

Bean Curd
This is made from soy beans, usually not used in Pritikin cuisine. However, for vegetarians bean curd is an excellent source of protein. Three ounces (100g) of bean curd per day can be used. Fresh bean curd is preferable. Before using drain and rinse with cold water each day to help it last longer.

Bean Sprouts
The most popular sprouts used in Chinese cuisine are mung or soy bean sprouts. Make sure the fresh sprouts you buy are clean and white — a sure sign of freshness. Rinse with water each day and keep in the refrigerator.

Black Beans
These are soy beans, and should be used in small quantities as they tend to be salty. Soak in cold water for 15 minutes to help remove excess salt. Rinse, drain and mash before using.

Chinese Beans
Sometimes called snake beans. They are very long and the two varieties are light and dark. The darker ones are considered to have more flavour. They can be substituted with ordinary French green beans.

Chinese Cabbage
There are many varieties including bok choy, gai choy, tientsin, mustard, bamboo

mustard and flowering cabbage. They are delicious shredded and eaten raw, or steamed, braised or blanched.

Chinese Chives
Similar to ordinary chives, but the taste is slightly stronger. They are also more fibrous. Use in soups and salads.

Chinese Melons
There are several varieties including bitter, fuzzy, and winter melons. The dark green winter melon is especially popular.

Chinese Mushrooms
The dried flower or winter mushrooms are delicious. Flower mushrooms are thicker and more expensive. Always soak dried Chinese mushrooms in hot water for 30 minutes before use. Discard stems. Straw mushrooms have a stronger flavour and their small caplike shape means they are often eaten whole. Available fresh or in cans.

Chinese Noodles
Fresh rich noodles are best. Dried rice noodles can be used. If you want to stick to the wholewheat variety choose the stoneground noodles available in some supermarkets and health food stores. Transparent pea starch noodles — also called bean threads or vermicelli — are popular too. Avoid the fresh dark yellow noodles — they are usually made with duck eggs.

Chinese Spinach
Has oval leaves and is usually sold with the roots attached. Some varieties have crimson centres. Discard roots and cook the same way as ordinary spinach.

Chinese Wine
This is made from rice and there are many varieties — sweet and dry. Ordinary dry or sweet sherry can be substituted. Do not use excessive quantities.

Coriander
This looks like flat-leaved parsley, but has its own special fragrance and flavour. Also makes an attractive garnish. Essential for a good Chinese vegetable stock.

Dried Tiger Lily Buds
These add a delicate flavour, but need to be soaked in hot water for 30 minutes. Lily buds are sometimes called golden needles.

Five Spice Powder
An aromatic blend of five spices: star anise, anise pepper, cloves, cinnamon and fennel. Available in powdered form, or you can grind your own.

Fresh Ginger
This is from the ginger root, and is essential for Chinese cooking. Powdered ginger

is a poor substitute. The preserved ginger tends to be loaded with salt, sugar and preservatives. Keep in the refrigerator. The Chinese also believe in the curative qualities of fresh ginger.

Garlic

Use only fresh garlic. Garlic powder and flakes can be substituted, but for authenticity stick to the fresh variety. Use according to taste. The Chinese believe garlic also has excellent medical properties.

Lotus Roots

Look out for the fresh ones. The dried variety can also be used. Soak in hot water for 20 minutes. Dried lotus leaves can be used for wrapping foods which can then be steamed.

Mangetout (Snow Peas)

Flat oval-shaped pea pods — a delicious colourful addition to Chinese food. Cook by blanching or lightly steaming.

Onions

We recommend using shallots or ordinary white onions.

Oriental Radish

This long white vegetable adds flavour and crispness to many Chinese recipes. It is delicious eaten raw or cooked.

Sesame Seeds

Not strictly Pritikin. However, used in small quantities these tiny seeds add a flavoursome nutty taste. If you are on the Pritikin Regression diet, avoid altogether. Flavour is enhanced if they are lightly toasted before use.

Soy Sauce

Fundamental to Chinese cuisine. However, most soy sauces are too salty. Use only low-salt soy sauce. This can be diluted even further with water or lemon juice. Light and dark soy sauces are available. Dark soy has a slightly stronger flavour.

Spring Roll Wrappers

Many of the commercial varieties are made with eggs. However, some are made with flour, water and salt. You can make your own using stoneground flour and water. Filo pastry can be substituted.

Star Anise

A red-brown, flower-shaped pod. Used in red cooked dishes. Has an aniseed taste.

Szechuan Peppercorns

A fragrant Chinese pepper which is aromatic rather than hot. Used to make up five spice powder. When freshly ground pepper is required these peppercorns add a real oriental flavour to the recipe.

Tangerine Peel
The dried skin of tangerines — an excellent ingredient for adding flavour to dishes. Before using dried tangerine peel soak in hot water for 20 minutes, rinse and drain. Substitute with fresh orange, lemon, lime or mandarin peel.

Vinegar
Various vinegars can be used. White vinegar is best for sweet and sour dishes. Chinese rice vinegar has a milder flavour. Brown rice vinegar is another flavoursome mild Chinese vinegar.

Water Chestnuts
These are delightfully crunchy, and don't hesitate to buy them if you see fresh ones. The canned ones tend to be salty. Rinse canned variety before use.

Watercress
An excellent garnish, and great for Chinese soups and salads. Available in good fruit and vegetable shops and markets.

Wonton Wrappers
Fresh rich noodle dough rolled into flat small squares. Wrap up mixed vegetables and lightly steam or drop into clear soups.

Wood Fungus
Sometimes called cloud ears. This rather ghastly looking stuff adds texture to meals. Soak in warm water for 10 minutes before use. Excellent addition to spring rolls.

HANDY HINTS FOR SUCCESSFUL PRITIKIN-STYLE CHINESE COOKING

- When shredded vegetables are required, shred with a chopper rather than a food blender. Flavour and texture are enhanced.
- Substitute canned bamboo shoots — with fresh if available.
- Be careful not to burn yourself with handles of bamboo cooking implements. During the cooking process they often become red hot. Always use a cooking mitt, or wrap a cloth around the handles.
- Cut vegetables and fruit a short time before cooking the meal to ensure they are as crisp and full of vitamins as possible. *Never* soak prepared vegetables in water, as this destroys valuable nutrients. Also never add bicarbonate of soda to retain colour. Overcooking vegetables is what destroys food colours.
- When stir frying in water, add a clove of chopped garlic and a sliver of chopped fresh ginger to flavour water.
- Place all cooked dishes on the table so people can help themselves. This is the traditional Chinese way to serve a meal.
- Jasmine or other herbal teas and fresh fruit slices are a pleasant way to complete a Chinese meal.
- The ratio of dishes is usually one main dish per head to one portion of rice.
- Ensure your wok doesn't wobble around the hot plate by placing it on a wok ring or stand.
- When cleaning Chinese utensils avoid using detergents as much as possible. They taint food. Hot running water is adequate.
- Ingredient freshness is a key to good Chinese cooking. Only select the freshest ingredients.
- When stir frying, always heat wok, frying-pan or saucepan before adding ingredients.
- When steaming food, with or without the lid on, make sure the dishes you place the food on are heatproof.

PLEASE NOTE:

All spoon measures are level.

Both metric and imperial measures are listed.

Recipes serve 4–6 unless otherwise stated.

CHINESE REGIONAL
COOKING STYLES

Chinese food is one of the world's most savoured and exotic cuisines, and China has at least nine different regional cooking styles. These include Peking, Fukien, Hunan, Szechuan and Canton.

The majority of Western restaurants serve either Cantonese or Peking-style food. Peking-style cuisine offers delicious sweet and sour sauces and Mongolian hot pot dishes.

Cantonese food includes dim sum, delicious noodle dishes and a wide variety of seasonings. Cantonese food tends to be lighter, with an emphasis on natural flavours.

If you like food to have plenty of 'zip', be spicy and sometimes very hot, Szechuan food is for you.

SOUPS & STARTERS

A wide variety of Chinese soups can be based on the Chinese basic vegetable stock recipe.

Remember, the Chinese do not think slurping soup is bad manners. Interesting Chinese garnishes perfect for floating on top of soups before serving include shallot curls, radish roses, carrot shapes produced by a decorative cutter, sprouts and strips of Chinese noodles and mushrooms.

Try non-greasy spring rolls! They're easy to make and delicious. You won't be able to stop at one!

I hope you enjoy the other delectable starters presented here, and the Chinese garnishes are easy and fun to make.

HOW TO MAKE GARNISHES
FOR CHINESE FOOD

Shallot Curls
Remove outer skin of shallot and trim both ends. Slice the green end into brush-like strips. Cut down about one inch (2.5cm) into the shallot. Place in iced water for 10 minutes until the shallot curls.

Carrot Cutouts
Peel carrot and cut into thin discs. With a special pastry cutter press into carrot disc; or you can carve your own shapes with a sharp knife. Flower petal shapes are attractive.

Lemon and Orange Twists
Cut a lemon and orange into thin discs. With a sharp knife cut disc through the middle up to white pith. Pull both ends of disc until it twists and place on your favourite vegetable dishes.

Radish Roses
Rinse radishes and with a sharp knife make small incisions all around the radish. Put in cold water until flower shape opens.

Fresh Flowers
Fresh rose petals, violets and other flowers can add an artistic touch to your Chinese meals. They look especially beautiful as a garnish with fresh fruit.

BASIC CHINESE VEGETABLE STOCK

Imperial (Metric)	**American**
1¼ lb (500g) mixed vegetables, roughly chopped	3 cups mixed vegetables, roughly chopped
2 garlic cloves, chopped	2 garlic cloves, chopped
1 tablespoon chopped fresh ginger	1 tablespoon chopped fresh ginger
1 medium white onion, roughly chopped	1 medium white onion, roughly chopped
3 pints (1.75 litres) water	6 cups water
Freshly ground pepper	Freshly ground pepper
1 carrot, roughly chopped	1 carrot, roughly chopped
4 coriander stalks	4 coriander stalks

Cover all ingredients with cold water and bring to the
boil. Simmer covered for 45 minutes very slowly to
produce a more concentrated flavour.
Drain off soup and place in refrigerator.
Ideal for stir fry water dishes.

Freeze stock for later use.

TOMATO AND LEEK EGGFLOWER SOUP

Imperial (Metric)	American
2 medium leeks, cut into thin slices	2 medium leeks, cut into thin slices
2 medium tomatoes, diced	2 medium tomatoes, diced
2¼ pints (1.25 litres) basic Chinese vegetable stock	5 cups basic Chinese vegetable stock
2 tablespoons Chinese wine or dry sherry	2 tablespoons Chinese wine or dry sherry
1 tablespoon low-salt soy sauce	1 tablespoon low-salt soy sauce
2 teaspoons cornflour	2 teaspoons cornflour
1 tablespoon cold water	1 tablespoon cold water
3 egg whites, lightly beaten	3 egg whites, lightly beaten
Freshly ground pepper	Freshly ground pepper

Place leeks, tomatoes and stock in a saucepan. Bring to the boil. Reduce heat and simmer for 15 minutes. Mix wine or sherry, soy sauce, cornflour and cold water. Add to saucepan. Pour beaten egg whites slowly into the soup. Stir once or twice. Season with pepper and serve.

SPINACH AND BEAN CURD SOUP

Imperial (Metric)	American
2¼ pints (1.25 litres) basic Chinese vegetable stock	5 cups basic Chinese vegetable stock
1¾ lb (750g) of bean curd, cut into cubes	2 cakes of bean curd, cut into cubes
1 lb (455g) fresh spinach, torn into pieces	1 pound fresh spinach, torn into pieces
1 tablespoon low-salt soy sauce	1 tablespoon low-salt soy sauce
Freshly ground pepper	Freshly ground pepper
2 shallots, finely chopped	2 shallots, finely chopped

Bring stock to the boil. Add bean curd and spinach.
Simmer gently for 10 minutes. Stir in soy sauce. Season
with pepper and serve. Garnish with shallots.

LETTUCE WITH CELLOPHANE NOODLE SOUP

Imperial (Metric)
2½ pints (1.5 litres) basic Chinese vegetable stock

1 lettuce, roughly chopped

4 dried Chinese mushrooms (Soaked in hot water for 30 minutes. Discard stems and cut into quarters.)

3½ oz (100g) cellophane noodles (Soaked in hot water for 15 minutes and drained.)

1 tablespoon low-salt soy sauce

Freshly ground pepper

Garnish:
Shallots, finely sliced

American
5 cups basic Chinese vegetable stock

1 lettuce, roughly chopped

4 dried Chinese mushrooms (Soaked in hot water for 30 minutes. Discard stems and cut into quarters.)

¾ cup cellophane noodles (Soaked in hot water for 15 minutes and drained.)

1 tablespoon low-salt soy sauce

Freshly ground pepper

Garnish:
Shallots, finely sliced

Bring vegetable stock to the boil. Add lettuce, mushrooms, and cellophane noodles and simmer for 15 minutes.

Stir in soy sauce. Season with pepper, garnish and serve.

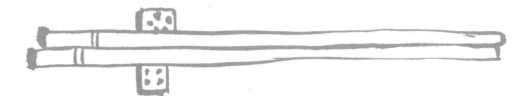

VEGETABLE COMBINATION SOUP

Imperial (Metric)

2 teaspoons fresh ginger, finely chopped

2½ pints (1.5 litres) basic Chinese vegetable stock

4 oz (115g) broccoli florets

½ lb (225g) spinach leaves, roughly chopped

½ lb (225g) Chinese cabbage, diced

4 oz (115g) mangetout peas, trimmed

4 dried Chinese mushrooms (Soaked in hot water for 30 minutes. Discard stems and slice into quarters.)

5 shallots, diced

4 oz (115g) vermicelli — bean threads. (Soaked in hot water for 30 minutes, drained and cut into medium lengths.)

13 oz (375g) fresh bean curd, cut into 12 pieces

Freshly ground pepper

1 tablespoon fresh coriander, chopped

American

2 teaspoons finely chopped fresh ginger

5 cups basic Chinese vegetable stock

1 cup broccoli flowerets

8 ounces spinach leaves, roughly chopped

2 cups Chinese cabbage, diced

¼ cup snow peas, trimmed

4 dried Chinese mushrooms (Soaked in hot water for 30 minutes. Discard stems and slice into quarters.)

5 shallots, diced

¾ cup vermicelli — bean threads. (Soaked in hot water for 30 minutes, drained and cut into medium lengths.)

1 cake fresh bean curd, cut into 12 pieces

Freshly ground pepper

1 tablespoon fresh coriander, chopped

Add ginger to the stock and bring to the boil in a large saucepan. Add vegetables to the stock. Bring to the boil, reduce heat and simmer for 30 minutes. Add bean thread noodles and bean curd and simmer for 2 minutes. Season with pepper, garnish with fresh coriander and serve.

WEST LAKE WATERCRESS SOUP

Imperial (Metric)	**American**
3 pints (1.75 litres) basic Chinese vegetable stock	*6 cups basic Chinese vegetable stock*
4 tablespoons Chinese wine or dry sherry	*¼ cup Chinese wine or dry sherry*
2 teaspoons low-salt soy sauce	*2 teaspoons low-salt soy sauce*
Freshly ground pepper	*Freshly ground pepper*
3 egg whites, lightly beaten	*3 egg whites, lightly beaten*
1½ oz (45g) watercress	*1½ cups fresh watercress*
2 teaspoons sesame seeds	*2 teaspoons sesame seeds*
3 shallots, diced	*3 shallots, diced*

Bring stock to the boil and add wine or sherry, soy sauce and pepper. Reduce heat. Whisk through egg whites and watercress. When egg mixture turns white serve immediately. Sprinkle with sesame seeds and shallots.

HOT AND SOUR SOUP

Imperial (Metric)	**American**
2½ pints (1.5 litres) basic Chinese vegetable stock	5 cups basic Chinese vegetable stock
6 dried Chinese mushrooms (Soaked in hot water for 30 minutes. Discard stems and slice.)	6 dried Chinese mushrooms (Soaked in hot water for 30 minutes. Discard stems and slice.)
1 fresh red chilli, chopped	1 fresh red chili, chopped
1 tablespoon fresh ginger, finely chopped	1 tablespoon finely chopped fresh ginger
8 oz (225g) fresh bean curd, diced	1 cup fresh diced bean curd
1 tablespoon cloud ear mushrooms (Soaked in hot water for 10 minutes. Remove tough outer parts.)	1 tablespoon cloud ears (Soaked in hot water for 10 minutes. Remove tough bits.)
1 tablespoon low-salt soy sauce	1 tablespoon low-salt soy sauce
1 tablespoon Chinese wine or dry sherry	1 tablespoon Chinese wine or dry sherry
2 tablespoons vinegar	2 tablespoons vinegar
1 tablespoon cornflour mixed with 1 tablespoon of cold water	1 tablespoon cornflour mixed with 1 tablespoon of cold water
3 egg whites, lightly beaten	3 egg whites, lightly beaten
Freshly ground pepper	Freshly ground pepper
2 shallots, sliced	2 shallots, sliced

Bring stock to the boil. Add Chinese mushrooms, chilli and ginger. Reduce heat, cover and simmer for 5 minutes. Add bean curd, cloud ears, soy sauce, wine or sherry and vinegar. Simmer for 2 minutes.

Pour cornflour mixture into soup and bring to the boil for 1 minute. Remove from heat and swirl through egg whites. Season with pepper and garnish with shallots.

MONGOLIAN HOT POT
Serves 8

Imperial (Metric)	American
4 pints (2.25 litres) basic Chinese vegetable stock	8 cup basic Chinese vegetable stock
11 oz (310g) broccoli florets	2½ cups broccoli flowerets
11 oz (310g) cauliflower florets	2½ cups cauliflower flowerets
14 oz (395g) spinach, trimmed and roughly chopped	13 ounces spinach, trimmed and roughly chopped
14 oz (395g) Chinese cabbage, roughly chopped	13 ounces Chinese cabbage, roughly chopped
1 large lettuce, roughly chopped	1 large lettuce, roughly chopped
4½ oz (120g) rice vermicelli (Soaked in hot water for 20 minutes and drained.)	1 cup vermicelli (Soaked in hot water for 20 minutes and drain.)
4½ oz (120g) cellophane — bean thread noodles (Soaked in hot water for 20 minutes, drained and cut into short lengths.)	1 cup cellophane — bean thread noodles (Soaked in hot water for 20 minutes, drained and cut into short lengths.)
1 lb (455g) fresh bean curd (Soaked in hot water for 10 minutes, drained and diced.)	2 cakes fresh bean curd (Soaked in hot water for 10 minutes, drained and diced.)

This dish is traditionally cooked at the table in a charcoal heated fire pot. If a firepot is unavailable then a heatproof bowl and gas burner, or electric frypan can be used. The joy of this dish is that any fresh ingredients can be used. The list of ingredients should serve only as an outline. Use any seasonal vegetables.

Bring the stock to the boil on the stove and transfer 6 cups to the firepot. Keep it at boiling point by placing hot coals in the base of the firepot. Each person cooks his own portion of vegetables using either a wire spoon or chopsticks. Various sauces — soy, chilli, ginger or mustard should be placed in small containers in front of each person. Dip food into sauces prior to eating. When all the vegetables have been devoured put rice vermicelli, bean thread noodles and bean curd into the simmering rich stock. Add remaining stock. Cover and simmer for 10 minutes. Then enjoy the delectable flavours of this amazing soup to round off your Mongolian hot pot/steamboat meal.

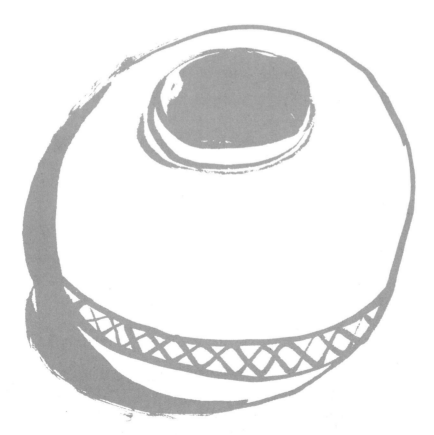

SPRING ROLLS

Imperial (Metric)

12 spring roll wrappers. Filo pastry sheets cut into squares can be used.

Filling:
2 cloves garlic, finely chopped
2 teaspoons ginger, finely chopped
3 tablespoons basic Chinese vegetable stock
4 shallots, finely diced
1 lb (455g) cabbage, finely shredded
8 oz (225g) bean sprouts
4 dried Chinese mushrooms (Soaked in hot water for 30 minutes. Discard stems and slice.)
1 red chilli, finely chopped
1 tablespoon low-salt soy salt
2 tablespoons Chinese wine or dry sherry
2 teaspoons cornflour
Freshly ground pepper

American

12 spring roll wrappers. Filo pastry sheets cut into squares can be used.

Filling:
2 cloves garlic, finely chopped
2 teaspoons ginger, finely chopped
3 tablespoons basic Chinese vegetable stock
4 shallots, finely diced
1 pound finely shredded cabbage
7 ounces (3½ cups) bean sprouts
4 dried Chinese mushrooms (Soaked in hot water for 30 minutes. Discard stems and slice.)
1 red chili, finely chopped
1 tablespoon low-salt soy sauce
2 tablespoons Chinese wine or dry sherry
2 teaspoons cornflour
Freshly ground pepper

Add garlic and ginger to wok or non-stick frying-pan. Stir fry for 1 minute with 1 tablespoon of stock. Add shallots, cabbage, bean sprouts, mushrooms and chilli to frying-pan. Stir for 2 minutes with remaining stock.

Mix soy sauce, wine or sherry, cornflour and pepper. Add to pan and simmer for 1 minute. Allow to cool. Drain off excess liquid. Divide mixture into 12 portions. Place each portion in centre of spring roll wrapper. Fold over sides and roll into envelope shaped parcel. Preheat oven to 200°C–400°F and bake for 30 minutes until golden brown.

Serve with a dipping sauce.

SOY SAUCE LOTUS ROOT

Imperial (Metric)	**American**
1 lb (455g) fresh lotus root	*2¾ cups fresh lotus root. (If*
(If unavailable use dried lotus root.)	*unavailable use dried lotus root.)*
Marinade:	**Marinade:**
2 tablespoons low-salt soy sauce	*2 tablespoons low-salt soy sauce*
1 teaspoon vinegar	*1 teaspoon vinegar*
4 tablespoons fresh orange juice	*¼ cup fresh orange juice*
1 teaspoon chopped fresh ginger	*1 teaspoon chopped fresh ginger*
1 garlic clove, chopped	*1 garlic clove, chopped*
Freshly ground pepper	*Freshly ground pepper*
Garnish:	**Garnish:**
1 teaspoon toasted sesame seeds	*1 teaspoon toasted sesame seeds*

Peel lotus root and trim off ends of root. Rinse in cold water and drain. Cut the lotus root into thick slices. If using dried lotus root, soak in hot water for 20 minutes. Rinse and drain. Combine marinade ingredients in a bowl. Add lotus root and marinate for 1 hour.

Drain lotus root, reserve marinade and bring to the boil in wok or frying-pan. Add lotus root and stir fry for 4 minutes. Remove from heat. Sprinkle with sesame seeds and serve.

RED COOKED EGGPLANT

Imperial (Metric)	American
2 medium-sized aubergines	2 medium-sized eggplants
⅔ pint (340ml) basic Chinese vegetable stock	1½ cups basic Chinese vegetable stock
1 tablespoon fresh ginger, chopped	1 tablespoon fresh ginger, chopped
1 clove garlic, chopped	1 clove garlic, chopped
2 tablespoons low-salt soy sauce	2 tablespoons low-salt soy sauce
1 tablespoon fresh orange juice	1 tablespoon fresh orange juice

Remove stems from aubergines and cut into thick slices, then into thick strips. Bring stock to the boil and add aubergine slices. Stir fry with ginger and garlic for 3 minutes. Reduce heat, and add soy sauce and orange juice. Simmer for another 3 minutes. Remove aubergines from pan and drain.

VEGETABLES WRAPPED IN LOTUS LEAVES

Imperial (Metric)	American
1 oz (30g) chopped dried tangerine peel	¼ cup chopped dried tangerine peel
¾ lb (340g) cooked brown rice	2 cups cooked brown rice
8 dried Chinese mushrooms (Soaked for 30 minutes in hot water. Discard stems and slice.)	8 dried Chinese mushrooms (Soaked for 30 minutes in hot water. Discard stems and slice.)
¾ lb (340g) finely diced mixed vegetables — bean sprouts, bamboo shoots, carrot, celery, cabbage	2 cups finely diced mixed vegetables — bean sprouts, bamboo shoots, carrot, celery, cabbage
1 tablespoon low-salt soy sauce	1 tablespoon low-salt soy sauce
4 fl oz (120ml) basic Chinese vegetable stock	½ cup basic Chinese vegetable stock
1 clove garlic, chopped	1 clove garlic, chopped
1 teaspoon finely chopped fresh ginger	1 teaspoon finely chopped fresh ginger
1 tablespoon toasted sesame seeds	1 tablespoon toasted sesame seeds
3 large dried lotus leaves (Soaked in warm water for 15 minutes. Drain on absorbent paper.)	3 large dried lotus leaves (Soaked in warm water for 15 minutes. Drain on absorbent paper.)

Soak tangerine peel in hot water for 20 minutes and drain. Combine tangerine peel with all other ingredients except lotus leaves. Let stand in a cool place for 1 hour.

Cut lotus leaves in half. Stuff small quantity of mixture into each leaf segment and roll into a tight parcel. Secure with string and place in steamer for 10 minutes until heated through. Unwrap parcels at the table and serve.

BROCCOLI IN GINGER SOY SAUCE

Imperial (Metric)
4 fl oz (120ml) water
¾ lb (340g) broccoli florets

American
½ cup water
3 cups broccoli flowerets

Sauce:
2 teaspoons cornflour
1 tablespoon low-salt soy sauce
4 fl oz (120ml) basic Chinese vegetable stock
1 tablespoon fresh ginger, chopped
Freshly ground pepper
Squeeze of lemon juice

Sauce:
2 teaspoons cornflour
1 tablespoon low-salt soy sauce
½ cup basic Chinese vegetable stock
1 tablespoon fresh ginger, chopped
Freshly ground pepper
Squeeze of lemon juice

Bring water to the boil and stir fry broccoli for 2 minutes. Remove from wok or frying-pan. Combine cornflour with stock. Add to remaining sauce ingredients and bring to the boil. Reduce heat and simmer for 2 minutes until sauce thickens. Stir continuously.
Pour over broccoli and serve.

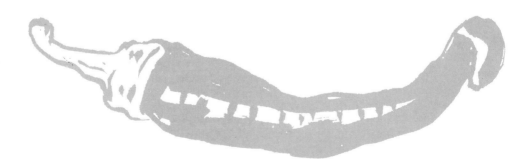

STEAMED STUFFED MUSHROOMS WITH CHILLI

Imperial (Metric)	American
1 tablespoon cornflour	*1 tablespoon cornflour*
6 oz (170g) par-boiled brown rice	*1 cup par-boiled brown rice*
1 stick celery, finely diced	*1 stick finely diced celery*
2 fresh red chillies, finely chopped	*2 fresh red chilis, finely chopped*
1 teaspoon garlic, finely chopped	*1 teaspoon finely chopped garlic*
1 teaspoon fresh ginger, finely chopped	*1 teaspoon finely chopped fresh ginger*
1 teaspoon low-salt soy sauce	*1 teaspoon low-salt soy sauce*
1 teaspoon Chinese wine or dry sherry	*1 teaspoon Chinese wine or dry sherry*
1 egg white, lightly beaten	*1 egg white, lightly beaten*
½ teaspoon sesame seeds	*½ teaspoon sesame seeds*
12 dried Chinese mushrooms (Soaked for 30 minutes in hot water. Discard stems.)	*12 dried Chinese mushrooms (Soaked for 30 minutes in hot water. Discard stems.)*

Sprinkle cornflour over all ingredients except mushrooms. Then mix everything together and let stand for 30 minutes. Stuff small quantity of mixture into each mushroom. Place mushrooms on heatproof dish and put into steamer with lid on. Steam over a gentle heat for 15 minutes.
Serve hot.

CHINESE VEGETABLE CRUDITÉS

Imperial (Metric)	American
4 oz (115g) broccoli florets	1 cup broccoli flowerets
4 oz (115g) cauliflower florets	1 cup cauliflower flowerets
2 carrots, cut into thin strips	2 carrots, cut into thin strips
4 dried Chinese mushrooms (Soaked for 30 minutes in hot water. Discard stems. Steam for 10 minutes and slice in half.)	4 dried Chinese mushroom (Soaked for 30 minutes in hot water. Discard stems. Steam for 10 minutes and slice in half.)
1 cucumber, sliced	1 cucumber, sliced
4 shallots, trimmed and ends cut into tassels	4 shallot curls
6 radish roses	6 radish roses
2 cloves garlic, chopped	2 cloves garlic, chopped
1 tablespoon fresh ginger, chopped	1 tablespoon chopped fresh ginger
4 tablespoons low-salt soy sauce	¼ cup low-salt soy sauce
1 tablespoon toasted sesame seeds	1 tablespoon toasted sesame seeds
Squeeze of lemon juice	Squeeze of lemon juice

Arrange vegetables decoratively on serving plate.
Combine remaining ingredients to make a dipping
sauce. Serve with vegetables.

GREAT WALL STUFFED GREEN OR RED PEPPERS

Imperial (Metric)	American
1 medium white onion, diced	1 medium white onion, diced
1 clove garlic, chopped	1 clove garlic, chopped
1 teaspoon fresh ginger, chopped	1 teaspoon chopped fresh ginger
2 tablespoons water	2 tablespoons water
1 lb (455g) cooked minced bean curd	2 cups cooked minced bean curd
1 carrot, grated	1 carrot, grated
1 tablespoon low-salt soy sauce	1 tablespoon low-salt soy sauce
Freshly ground pepper	Freshly ground pepper
½ teaspoon five spice powder	½ teaspoon five spice powder
3 green or red peppers, cut into quarters	3 green or red capsicums, cut into quarters
Squeeze of lemon juice	Squeeze of lemon juice

Stir fry onion, garlic and ginger in water over high heat until tender, about 2 minutes. Add to bean curd, carrot, soy sauce, pepper and five spice powder. Mix to combine well. Remove seeds and pith from peppers. Stuff equal amount of mixture into each quarter. Place on non-stick baking tray and cook in oven preheated to 200°C/400°F (Gas Mark 6) for 10 minutes.

Remove from oven and sprinkle with lemon juice. Garnish with thin strips of extra red and green peppers.

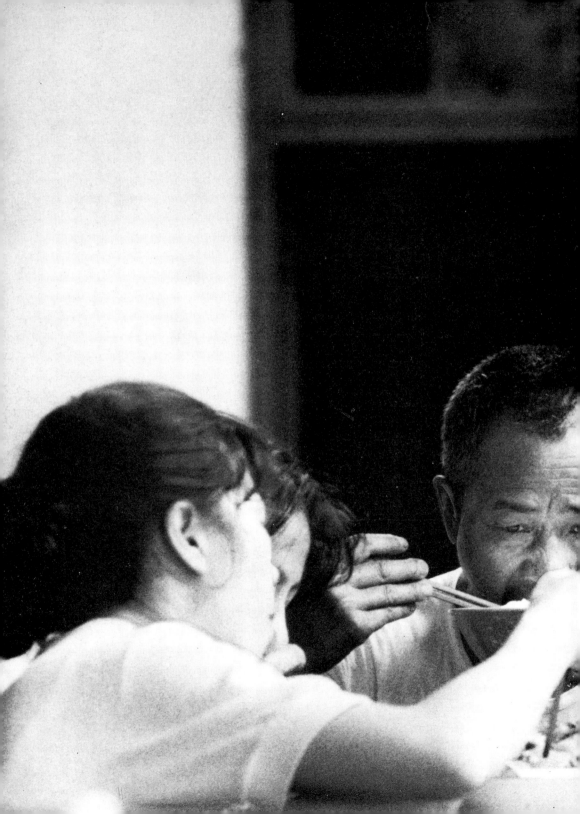

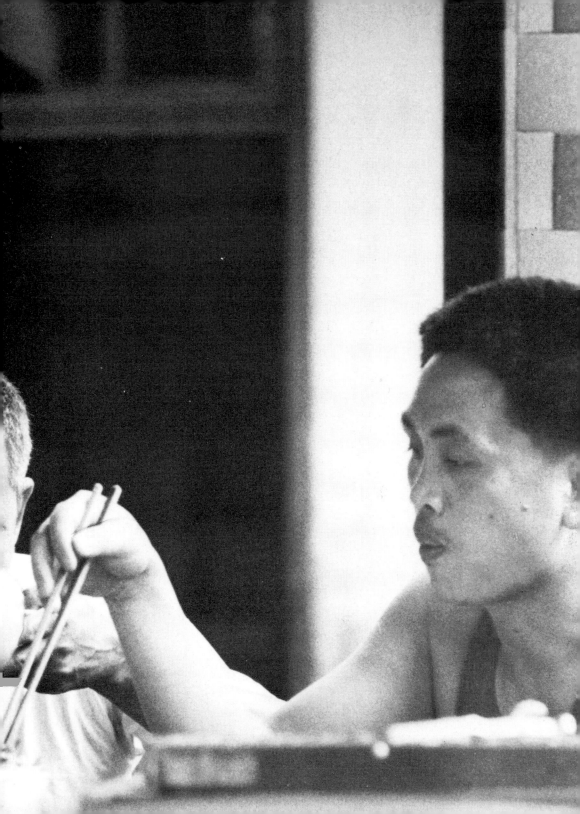

PICKLED BOK CHOY

Imperial (Metric)	**American**
1 lb (455g) bok choy (Chinese cabbage) (Remove leaves and chop stems into short lengths.)	*1 pound bok choy (Chinese cabbage) (Remove leaves and chop stems into short lengths.)*
18 fl oz (500ml) cider vinegar	*2 cups cider vinegar*
2 tablespoons fresh ginger, finely chopped	*2 tablespoons finely chopped fresh ginger*
1 tablespoon black peppercorns	*1 tablespoon black peppercorns*
1 red chilli, finely chopped	*1 red chili, finely chopped*

Blanch bok choy in boiling water for 2 minutes. Drain and set aside.

Add remaining ingredients to saucepan and simmer for 5 minutes. Pour contents of saucepan over bok choy, cover and refrigerate for 3 days.
Serve cold.

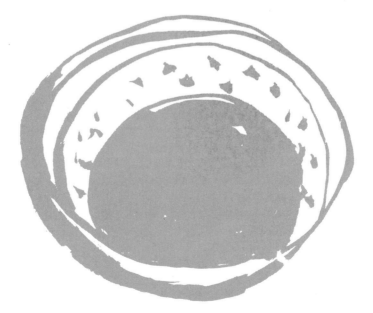

Chinese Vegetable Crudités
(page 44).

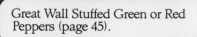

Great Wall Stuffed Green or Red
Peppers (page 45).

Hot Turnip Soup (page 51).

Mangetout (Snow Peas) with
Cucumber (page 69).

BRAISED COMBINATION MUSHROOMS

Imperial (Metric)	American
4 oz (115g) dried Chinese mushrooms (Soaked in hot water for 30 minutes. Discard stems and cut into quarters.)	1½ cups dried Chinese mushrooms (Soaked in hot water for 30 minutes. Discard stems and cut into quarters.)
7 oz (200g) straw mushrooms, rinsed and drained	3½ cups straw mushrooms, rinsed and drained
4 oz (115g) field mushrooms, trimmed and sliced	1½ cups field mushrooms, trimmed and sliced
3 tablespoons basic Chinese vegetable stock	3 tablespoons basic Chinese vegetable stock
2 teaspoons fresh ginger, finely chopped	2 teaspoons finely chopped fresh ginger
3 shallots, finely chopped	2 shallots, finely chopped
2 tablespoons Chinese wine or dry sherry	2 tablespoons Chinese wine or dry sherry
1 tablespoon low-salt soy sauce	1 tablespoon low-salt soy sauce
1 teaspoon cornflour	1 teaspoon cornflour
Freshly ground pepper	Freshly ground pepper

Stir fry mushroom combination in a non-stick frying-pan in 2 tablespoons of vegetable stock for 3 minutes with ginger and shallots.

Mix remaining stock, soy sauce and sherry with the cornflour. Add to mushroom combination. Reduce heat and simmer for 2 minutes.

Season with pepper and serve.

PEASANT ASPARAGUS SOUP

Imperial (Metric)	American
1¾ pints (1 litre) basic Chinese vegetable stock	4 cups basic Chinese vegetable stock
16 fresh asparagus spears, trimmed and cut into short lengths	16 fresh asparagus spears, trimmed and cut into short lengths
1 tablespoon Chinese wine or sherry	1 tablespoon Chinese wine or sherry
2 tablespoons cornflour mixed with 4 tablespoons cold water	2 tablespoons cornflour mixed with 4 tablespoons cold water
Freshly ground pepper	Freshly ground pepper
4 egg whites, lightly beaten	4 egg whites, lightly beaten

Bring stock to the boil. Add asparagus and boil for 10 minutes. Add Chinese wine or sherry, cornflour mixture and pepper. Cover and simmer for 10 minutes. Swirl through egg whites. Simmer for 5 minutes and serve.

HOT TURNIP SOUP

Imperial (Metric)

2½ pints (1.5 litres) basic Chinese vegetable stock

1 lb (455g) turnips, finely chopped

2 cloves garlic

1 fresh red or green chilli, finely chopped

1 tablespoon fresh ginger, chopped

3 tablespoons cornflour mixed with 4 tablespoons cold water

3 egg whites, lightly beaten

Freshly ground pepper

Garnish:

3 oz (85g) shallots, sliced

American

6 cups basic Chinese vegetable stock

1 pound (3 cups) turnips, finely chopped

2 cloves garlic

1 fresh red or green chili, finely chopped

1 tablespoon finely chopped fresh ginger

3 tablespoons cornflour mixed with 4 tablespoons cold water

3 egg whites, lightly beaten

Freshly ground pepper

Garnish:

½ cup sliced shallots

Bring stock to the boil and add turnips, garlic, chilli and ginger. Cover and simmer for 30 minutes. Purée in blender. Return to saucepan. Add cornflour mixture, egg whites and pepper. Simmer for a further 5 minutes. Garnish and serve.

MELON SOUP

Imperial (Metric)	American
1 medium-sized winter melon	1 medium-sized winter melon
2½ pints (1.5 litres) basic Chinese vegetable stock	6 cups basic Chinese vegetable stock
2 cloves garlic, chopped	2 cloves garlic, chopped
1 tablespoon Chinese wine or dry sherry	1 tablespoon Chinese wine or dry sherry
6 dried Chinese mushrooms (Soaked in hot water for 30 minutes. Discard stems and slice.)	6 dried Chinese mushrooms (Soaked in hot water for 30 minutes. Discard stems and slice.)
1 tablespoon low-salt soy sauce	1 tablespoon low-salt soy sauce
Freshly ground pepper	Freshly ground pepper

Peel the melon. Discard seeds and cut into small chunks. Bring stock to the boil, add all ingredients and simmer for 20 minutes.

PRITIKIN-STYLE CHINESE DIPPING SAUCES

These delicious dipping sauces are ideal accompaniments to spring rolls, Mongolian hot pot meals, stuffed mushrooms, vegetable crudités, and many more. The fresh ingredients used make these sauces especially tasty.

GINGER DIP

Imperial (Metric)	American
2 tablespoons low-salt soy sauce	2 tablespoons low-salt soy sauce
1 tablespoon ginger, finely chopped	1 tablespoon ginger, finely chopped

Combine and serve.

CHINESE WINE OR DRY SHERRY DIP

Imperial (Metric)	American
4 tablespoons low-salt soy sauce	4 tablespoons low-salt soy sauce
1 tablespoon Chinese wine or dry sherry	1 tablespoon Chinese wine or dry sherry

Combine and serve.

CHILLI DIP

Imperial (Metric)
4 tablespoons low-salt soy sauce
1 fresh red chilli, finely sliced

American
4 tablespoons low-salt soy sauce
1 fresh red chili, finely sliced

Combine and serve.

MUSTARD DIP

Imperial (Metric)
4 tablespoons low-salt soy sauce
1 tablespoon Dijon mustard

American
4 tablespoons low-salt soy sauce
1 tablespoon Dijon mustard

Combine and serve.

SESAME DIP

Imperial (Metric)
1 tablespoon low-salt soy sauce
2 teaspoons toasted sesame seeds

American
1 tablespoon low-salt soy sauce
2 teaspoons toasted sesame seeds

Combine and serve.

LEMON DIP

Imperial (Metric)
4 tablespoons low-salt soy sauce
1 tablespoon fresh lemon juice

American
4 tablespoons low-salt soy sauce
1 tablespoon fresh lemon juice

Combine and serve.

PINEAPPLE DIP

Imperial (Metric)
4 tablespoons low-salt soy sauce
*2 tablespoons unsweetened
pineapple juice*

American
4 tablespoons low-salt soy sauce
*2 tablespoons unsweetened
pineapple juice*

Combine and serve.

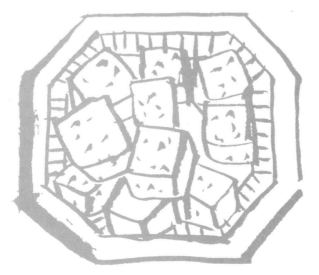

VEGETABLE DISHES

Vegetables cooked or raw Chinese style are a great taste sensation. The extensive range of vegetables available provides enormous scope for succulent oriental vegetable dishes.

If you haven't already discovered lotus roots, bean sprouts, water chestnuts, bamboo shoots, mangetout (snow peas) and Chinese mushrooms you're in for a treat.

Choose a selection of these to make up a main course or individually as side dishes.

PEPPERS IN BLACK BEAN SAUCE

Imperial (Metric)	**American**
4 fl oz (120ml) basic Chinese vegetable stock	½ cup basic Chinese vegetable stock
1 clove garlic, chopped	1 clove garlic, chopped
6 medium green or red peppers, trimmed and cut into thin strips	6 medium green or red peppers, trimmed and cut into thin strips
1 tablespoon black beans (Soaked in cold water for 15 minutes to remove excess salt. Rinse, drain and mash.)	1 tablespoon black beans (Soaked in cold water for 15 minutes to remove excess salt. Rinse, drain and mash.)
1 tablespoon soy sauce	1 tablespoon soy sauce
Freshly ground pepper	Freshly ground pepper

Bring stock to the boil. Add garlic and pepper strips.
Stir fry for 1 minute. Add black beans, soy sauce and
pepper and stir fry for 1 minute.

CHILLI BEAN CURD

Imperial (Metric)	American
8 fl oz (240ml) basic Chinese vegetable stock	1 cup basic Chinese vegetable stock
1 lb (455g) fresh bean curd, cubed	2 cups fresh bean curd, cubed
2 tablespoons low-salt soy sauce	2 tablespoons low-salt soy sauce
4 shallots, sliced	4 shallots, sliced
2 teaspoons fresh ginger, finely chopped	2 teaspoons finely chopped fresh ginger
2 tablespoons Chinese wine or dry sherry	2 tablespoons Chinese wine or dry sherry
1 tablespoon vinegar	1 tablespoon vinegar
2 fresh red chillies, finely chopped	2 fresh red chilis, finely chopped
Freshly ground black pepper	Freshly ground black pepper
2 teaspoons cornflour mixed with 1 tablespoon cold water	2 teaspoons cornflour mixed with 1 tablespoon cold water

Bring stock to the boil and add all ingredients. Simmer for 5 minutes and serve. Garnish with extra sliced shallots.

BRAISED CHILLI RADISH

Imperial (Metric)	American
1 large white oriental radish	1 large white oriental radish
8 fl oz (240ml) basic Chinese vegetable stock	1 cup basic Chinese vegetable stock
2 teaspoons fresh ginger, finely chopped	2 teaspoons finely chopped fresh ginger
1 clove garlic, chopped	1 clove garlic, chopped
1 fresh red chilli, chopped	1 fresh red chili, chopped
6 oz (170g) shallots, diced	1 cup diced shallots
1 tablespoon Chinese wine or dry sherry	1 tablespoon Chinese wine or dry sherry
2 tablespoons low-salt soy sauce	2 tablespoons low-salt soy sauce
1 tablespoon cornflour mixed with 2 tablespoons cold water	1 tablespoon cornflour mixed with 2 tablespoons cold water
Freshly ground pepper	Freshly ground pepper

Peel and trim radish. Cut into thin slices. Bring stock
to the boil and add ginger, garlic and chilli. Add radish
and shallots and stir fry for 2–3 minutes. Add wine or
sherry, soy sauce, cornflour mixture and pepper.
Simmer for 2 minutes.

MANGETOUT (SNOW PEAS) WITH GARLIC

Imperial (Metric)	American
4 shallots, diced	*4 shallots, diced*
4 cloves garlic, chopped	*4 cloves garlic, chopped*
⅞ lb (340g) mangetout peas — trim ends	*4 cups snow peas — trim ends*
8 fl oz (240ml) basic Chinese vegetable stock	*1 cup basic Chinese vegetable stock*
2 tablespoons low-salt soy sauce	*2 tablespoons low-salt soy sauce*
Freshly ground black pepper	*Freshly ground black pepper*
2 teaspoons cornflour mixed with 1 tablespoon water	*2 teaspoons cornflour mixed with 1 tablespoon cold water*
1 tablespoon toasted sesame seeds	*1 tablespoon toasted sesame seeds*

Stir fry shallots, garlic and mangetout in a non stick frying-pan with 3 tablespoons vegetable stock for 2 minutes. Mix remaining vegetable stock with soy sauce, pepper and cornflour and add to pan. Simmer for 1 minute. Sprinkle with sesame seeds and serve.

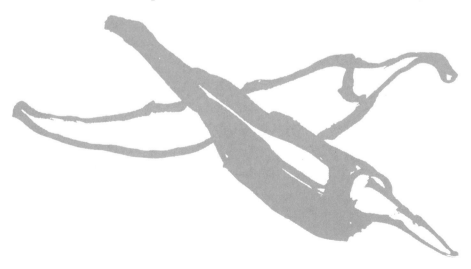

BRAISED TOMATOES AND SHALLOTS

Imperial (Metric)	**American**
1 lb (455g) ripe tomatoes	*2½ cups ripe tomatoes*
8 fl oz (250ml) basic Chinese vegetable stock	*1 cup basic Chinese vegetable stock*
6 shallots, diced	*6 shallots, diced*
1 tablespoon (15ml) low-salt soy sauce	*1 tablespoon low-salt soy sauce*
1½ teaspoons (7.5ml) cornflour mixed with 1 tablespoon (15ml) unsweetened orange juice	*2 teaspoons cornflour mixed with 1 tablespoon unsweetened orange*

Trim tomatoes and cut into small wedges. Bring stock to the boil. Add tomatoes and shallots. Cover and simmer for 5 minutes. Stir in soy sauce, cornflour mixed with orange juice and serve.

SWEET AND SOUR LOTUS ROOT

Imperial (Metric)	American
1 lb (455g) fresh lotus root. (Peel and trim ends of root. If using dried lotus root soak in hot water for 20 minutes. Rinse and drain.)	2¾ cups fresh lotus root. (Peel and trim ends of root. If using dried lotus root soak in hot water for 20 minutes. Rinse and drain.)
1 tablespoon vinegar	1 tablespoon vinegar
1 tablespoon low-salt soy sauce	1 tablespoon low-salt soy sauce
1 tablespoon unsweetened orange juice	1 tablespoon unsweetened orange juice
1 tablespoon unsweetened pineapple juice	1 tablespoon unsweetened pineapple juice
1 tablespoon unsweetened apple juice	1 tablespoon unsweetened apple juice
Freshly ground pepper	Freshly ground pepper
8 fl oz (240ml) basic Chinese vegetable stock	1 cup basic Chinese vegetable stock
2 teaspoons cornflour mixed with 1 tablespoon cold water	2 teaspoons cornflour mixed with 1 tablespoon cold water

Cut lotus root into thin strips. Marinate strips in vinegar, soy sauce, juices and pepper.

Bring stock to the boil. Add lotus root strips and stir fry for 2 minutes. Pour in marinade and cornflour mixture and simmer for another 4 minutes.

CELERY WITH BLACK BEAN SAUCE

Imperial (Metric)
2 cloves garlic, finely chopped

1 tablespoon black beans (Soak in cold water for 15 minutes to remove excess salt. Drain and mash.)

1 red chilli, finely chopped

3 tablespoons basic Chinese vegetable stock

½ lb (225g) celery, cut into thin slices

4 shallots, chopped diagonally into thin strips

2 oz (55g) bean sprouts

Sauce:
2 tablespoons basic Chinese vegetable stock

2 tablespoons Chinese wine or dry sherry

1 teaspoon cornflour

Freshly ground pepper

American
2 cloves garlic, finely chopped

1 tablespoon black beans (Soak in cold water for 15 minutes to remove excess salt. Drain and mash.)

1 red chili, finely chopped

3 tablespoons basic Chinese vegetable stock

2 cups celery, cut into thin slices

4 shallots, chopped diagonally into thin strips

1 cup bean sprouts

Sauce:
2 tablespoons basic Chinese vegetable stock

2 tablespoons Chinese wine or dry sherry

1 teaspoon cornflour

Freshly ground pepper

Add garlic, black beans and chilli to hot wok or non-stick frying-pan. Stir fry for 1 minute with 1 tablespoon of stock. Add celery, shallots, and bean sprouts and stir fry for 2 minutes with 2 tablespoons of stock.

Mix sauce ingredients. Add to wok and simmer for 1 minute until sauce thickens.

BEAN CURD WITH LILY BUDS AND SHALLOTS

Imperial (Metric)	American
25 dried lily buds (golden needles)	25 dried lily buds (golden needles)
4 fl oz (120ml) water	½ cup water
14 oz (400g) fresh bean curd, cubed	1¾ cups fresh bean curd, cubed
½ teaspoon fresh ginger, chopped	½ teaspoon chopped fresh ginger
3 oz (85g) shallots, finely sliced	½ cup finely sliced shallots

Sauce:	*Sauce:*
1 teaspoon cornflour	1 teaspoon cornflour
2 tablespoons water	2 tablespoons water
1 tablespoon low-salt soy sauce	1 tablespoon low-salt soy sauce
1 teaspoon Chinese wine or dry sherry	1 teaspoon Chinese wine or dry sherry
Freshly ground pepper	Freshly ground pepper

Soak the lily buds in hot water for 30 minutes and drain. Trim tough ends of lily buds. Bring water to the boil and stir fry ginger. Add bean curd and lily buds, reduce heat and simmer for 3 minutes.

To make sauce, combine cornflour with water, add soy sauce, wine and pepper and bring to the boil in small saucepan stirring continuously. Reduce heat and simmer for 1 minute until sauce thickens.

Remove bean curd from wok or frying-pan and spoon over sauce. Sprinkle with shallots and serve.

MELON WITH BAMBOO SHOOTS
AND SHALLOTS

Imperial (Metric)	American
1 medium-sized winter melon	*1 medium-sized winter melon*
4 fl oz (120ml) basic Chinese vegetable stock	*½ cup basic Chinese vegetable stock*
6 oz fresh or canned bamboo shoots	*1 cup sliced fresh or canned bamboo shoots*
1½ oz (45g) shallots, finely sliced	*¼ cup shallots, finely sliced*
1 clove garlic, chopped	*1 clove garlic, chopped*
½ teaspoon fresh ginger, chopped	*½ teaspoon fresh ginger, chopped*
1 teaspoon cornflour mixed with 1 tablespoon water	*1 teaspoon cornflour mixed with 1 tablespoon water*

Remove skin from melon and take out seeds and pulp.
Slice into bite-size pieces.

Bring stock to the boil and add all ingredients except
cornflour. Stir fry for 5 minutes. Thicken sauce with
cornflour mix, bring to the boil, reduce heat and stir
until sauce thickens.

Serve immediately.

PANDA BEAR BEAN CURD WITH MUSHROOMS

The day I tried this dish was also the day I saw
the famous Chinese panda bears at the Beijing (Peking)
Zoo.

Imperial (Metric)	American
2 cloves garlic, chopped	2 cloves garlic, chopped
½ teaspoon ginger, freshly chopped	½ teaspoon finely chopped fresh ginger
2 shallots, diced	2 shallots, diced
4 fl oz (120ml) basic Chinese vegetable stock	½ cup basic Chinese vegetable stock
13 oz (370g) fresh bean curd, cubed	1¾ cups fresh bean curd, cubed
4 oz (115g) broccoli florets	1 cup broccoli flowerets
2 oz (55g) dried Chinese mushrooms, sliced (Soak mushrooms in hot water for 30 minutes. Discard stems.)	1 cup dried Chinese mushrooms, sliced (Soak mushrooms in hot water for 30 minutes. Discard stems.)
1 tablespoon Chinese wine or dry sherry	1 tablespoon Chinese wine or dry sherry
2 teaspoons low-salt soy sauce	2 teaspoons low-salt soy sauce
2 teaspoons cornflour mixed with 1 tablespoon cold water	2 teaspoons cornflour mixed with 1 tablespoon cold water

Stir fry garlic, ginger and shallots in boiling stock until
tender, about 2 minutes. Add remaining ingredients
except cornflour mix and stir fry for 3–5 minutes. Be
careful not to break up bean curd. Add cornflour mix
and stir and simmer for 1 minute until sauce thickens.

Garnish with extra sliced shallots and serve.

MANGETOUT (SNOW PEAS) WITH CUCUMBER

Imperial (Metric)	American
4 fl oz (120ml) basic Chinese vegetable stock	½ cup basic Chinese vegetable stock
1 teaspoon fresh ginger, finely chopped	1 teaspoon finely chopped fresh ginger
2 cloves garlic, chopped	2 cloves garlic, chopped
8 oz (225g) mangetout, ends trimmed	2½ cups snow peas, ends trimmed
1 cucumber, finely sliced	1 cucumber, finely sliced
2 tablespoons low-salt soy sauce	2 tablespoons low-salt soy sauce

Bring stock to the boil. Add ginger, garlic, mangetout (snow peas) and cucumber. Stir fry in stock for 3–4 minutes. Sprinkle with soy sauce, garnish and serve.

EGG FOO YONG

Only egg whites are used in this recipe.

Imperial (Metric)	American
8 fl oz (240ml) basic Chinese vegetable stock	1 cup basic Chinese vegetable stock
6 dried mushrooms (Soaked for 30 minutes in hot water. Discard stems and slice.)	6 dried mushrooms (Soaked for 30 minutes in hot water. Discard stems and slice.)
3 shallots, finely sliced	3 shallots, finely sliced
10 water chestnuts, chopped	10 water chestnuts, chopped
2 oz (55g) fresh bean sprouts	1 cup fresh bean sprouts
6 oz (170g) bamboo shoots, sliced	1 cup bamboo shoots, sliced
2 tablespoons low-salt soy sauce	2 tablespoons low-salt soy sauce
7 egg whites	7 egg whites

Bring stock to the boil and add all ingredients except egg whites. Stir fry in stock for 5 minutes. Swirl through egg whites, simmer for 2 minutes and serve.

FRESH CORN, MANGETOUT (SNOW PEAS) AND CARROTS

Imperial (Metric)

4 fl oz (120ml) water

1 clove garlic, chopped

1 teaspoon (5ml) fresh ginger, chopped

¾ lb (340g) carrots, finely sliced

¾ lb (340g) fresh sweetcorn kernels

16 mangetout, ends trimmed

2 teaspoons (10ml) low-salt soy sauce

1 teaspoon (5ml) cornflour mixed with 1 tablespoon (15ml) cold water

Freshly ground pepper

American

½ cup water

1 clove garlic, chopped

1 teaspoon chopped fresh ginger

2 cups finely sliced carrots

2 cups fresh corn niblets

16 snow peas, trimmed

2 teaspoons low-salt soy sauce

1 teaspoon cornflour mixed with 1 tablespoon cold water

Freshly ground pepper

Bring water to the boil and stir fry garlic and ginger. Add carrots and corn and simmer and toss for 2 minutes. Add mangetout (snow peas). Stir in soy sauce. Thicken with cornflour mix. Simmer for 1 minute. Season with pepper and serve.

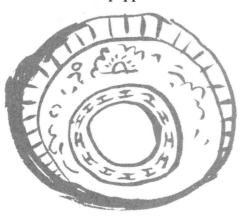

CARROTS WITH HOT PEPPER AND BLACK BEAN SAUCE

Imperial (Metric)

4 fl oz (120ml) water or stock

1½ tablespoons garlic, chopped

1½ lb (680g) carrots, cut into thin strips

1 tablespoon freshly ground Szechuan or black pepper

1 tablespoon black beans (Soak beans in cold water for 15 minutes to remove excess salt. Drain and mash.)

2 teaspoons Chinese wine or dry sherry

1 tablespoon cornflour mixed with 1 tablespoon cold water

American

½ cup water or stock

1½ tablespoons garlic, chopped

4 cups carrots, cut into thin strips

1 tablespoon freshly ground Szechuan or black pepper

1 tablespoon black beans (Soak beans in cold water for 15 minutes to remove excess salt. Drain and mash.)

2 teaspoons Chinese wine or dry sherry

1 tablespoon cornflour mixed with 1 tablespoon cold water

Bring water to the boil and stir fry garlic. Add carrots and stir fry for 3 minutes. Add all other ingredients and simmer for another 3 minutes. Thicken with cornflour mixed with water and simmer 1 minute.

PEKING PUMPKIN

Imperial (Metric)	American
8 fl oz (240ml) water or stock	1 cup water or stock
1¼ lb (565g) pumpkin, diced	3 cups pumpkin, diced
1 clove garlic, chopped	1 clove garlic, chopped
1 tablespoon fresh ginger, chopped	1 tablespoon fresh ginger, chopped
1 tablespoon low-salt soy sauce	1 tablespoon low-salt soy sauce
Freshly ground pepper	Freshly ground pepper
1 teaspoon cornflour mixed with 1 tablespoon cold water	1 teaspoon cornflour mixed with 1 tablespoon cold water
2 teaspoons toasted sesame seeds	2 teaspoons toasted sesame seeds

Bring water or stock to the boil and stir fry pumpkin for 15 minutes with garlic clove and ginger. Add soy sauce and pepper and simmer for another 2 minutes. Thicken with cornflour mix. Simmer for 1 minute.

Sprinkle with sesame seeds and serve.

STUFFED STEAMED PEPPERS IN MUSTARD SAUCE

Imperial (Metric)	American
6 small green or red peppers (Cut tops off and remove seeds.)	6 small green or red peppers (Cut tops off and remove seeds.)
Stuffing:	**Stuffing:**
6 oz (170g) cooked brown rice	1 cup cooked brown rice
1 shallot, finely chopped	1 shallot, finely chopped
1 tablespoon fresh ginger, finely chopped	1 tablespoon finely chopped fresh ginger
3 cloves garlic, finely chopped	3 cloves garlic, finely chopped
Freshly ground pepper	Freshly ground pepper
2 tablespoons Chinese wine or dry sherry	2 tablespoons Chinese wine or dry sherry
3 tablespoons basic Chinese vegetable stock	3 tablespoons basic Chinese vegetable stock
1 teaspoon cornflour	1 teaspoon cornflour
7 oz (200g) bean sprouts	3½ cups bean sprouts
Mustard sauce:	**Mustard sauce:**
1 tablespoon low-salt soy sauce	1 tablespoon low-salt soy sauce
1 tablespoon vinegar	1 tablespoon vinegar
2 teaspoons Dijon mustard	2 teaspoons Dijon mustard
2 tablespoons basic Chinese vegetable stock	2 tablespoons basic Chinese vegetable stock

---

Mix stuffing ingredients together except bean sprouts. Allow to stand for 15 minutes. Stir fry stuffing mixture in hot wok or frying-pan for 3 minutes. Add bean sprouts and stir fry for 2 minutes. Allow to cool. Stuff the peppers with the filling. Transfer stuffed peppers to steamer and steam vigorously on a plate for 10 minutes. Remove peppers from the plate. Mix mustard sauce ingredients with liquid on the plate. Pour over stuffed pepper and serve.

MUM'S BEAN CURD WITH FRESH CORIANDER SAUCE

Imperial (Metric)	**American**
1 lb (455g) fresh bean curd, cubed	2 cups fresh bean curd, cubed
1¼ pints (710ml) water	3 cups water
1 teaspoon fresh ginger, finely chopped	1 teaspoon finely chopped fresh ginger
2 cloves garlic, chopped	2 cloves garlic, chopped
Extra tablespoon water or stock	Extra tablespoon water or stock
2 tablespoons low-salt soy sauce	2 tablespoons low-salt soy sauce
1 tablespoon fresh orange juice	1 tablespoon fresh orange juice
½ oz coriander leaves, finely chopped	½ cup finely chopped coriander leaves

Rinse bean curd and drain. Bring water to the boil and simmer bean curd in it for 4 minutes. Remove from water and drain. Stir fry ginger and garlic in 1 tablespoon of water or stock for 2 minutes. Add soy sauce, orange juice and coriander. Pour over bean curd and serve.

WHITE COOKED CABBAGE WITH SWEET AND SOUR SAUCE

Imperial (Metric)	American
12 fl oz (340ml) basic Chinese vegetable stock	1½ cups basic Chinese vegetable stock
1 Chinese cabbage, shredded	1 Chinese cabbage, shredded
Sauce:	***Sauce:***
2 teaspoons vinegar	2 teaspoons vinegar
4 tablespoons fresh orange juice	4 tablespoons fresh orange juice
2 tablespoons unsweetened tomato juice	2 tablespoons unsweetened tomato juice
2 tablespoons Chinese wine or dry sherry	2 tablespoons Chinese wine or dry sherry
1 tablespoon cornflour	1 tablespoon cornflour

Bring stock to the boil. Add cabbage, cover and simmer for 10 minutes. Transfer cabbage to dish. Reserve stock. Mix sauce ingredients and bring to the boil. Add reserved stock. Reduce heat and simmer and stir for 2 minutes until sauce thickens. Spoon sauce over cabbage.

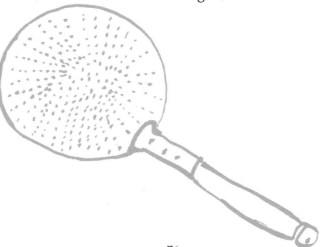

STEAMED AUBERGINE (EGGPLANT) WITH HOT GARLIC SAUCE

Imperial (Metric)	American
1 large aubergine, sliced into discs	*1 large eggplant sliced into discs*
Sauce:	***Sauce:***
6 cloves garlic, chopped	*6 cloves garlic, chopped*
3 tablespoons basic Chinese vegetable stock	*3 tablespoons basic Chinese vegetable stock*
1 fresh red chilli, finely chopped	*1 fresh red chili, finely chopped*
1 teaspoon cornflour	*1 teaspoon cornflour*
2 teaspoons low-salt soy sauce	*2 teaspoons low-salt soy sauce*
1 tablespoon Chinese wine or dry sherry	*1 tablespoon Chinese wine or dry sherry*
Freshly ground pepper	*Freshly ground pepper*

Place aubergine (eggplant) slices in a heatproof bowl.
Steam vigorously for 15 minutes. Stir fry garlic in 1
tablespoon of stock. Mix remaining sauce ingredients
and add to wok or frying-pan. Cover and simmer for 2
minutes. Remove aubergine (eggplant) from steamer.
Drain and spoon sauce over.

WHITE COOKED BEAN CURD AND TOMATOES

Imperial (Metric)	**American**
2 tomatoes, peeled and diced	2 tomatoes, peeled and diced
2 shallots, chopped	2 shallots, chopped
2 cloves garlic, chopped	2 cloves garlic, chopped
8 fl oz (240ml) basic Chinese vegetable stock	1 cup basic Chinese vegetable stock
2 tablespoons Chinese wine or dry sherry	2 tablespoons Chinese wine or dry sherry
½ lb (225g) fresh bean curd, cut into medium squares	1 cup fresh bean curd, cut into medium squares
Freshly ground pepper	Freshly ground pepper
2 teaspoons cornflour mixed with 1 tablespoon cold water	2 teaspoons cornflour mixed with 1 tablespoon cold water
1 tablespoon coriander leaves, chopped	1 tablespoon fresh coriander leaves, chopped

Stir fry tomatoes, shallots and garlic in a wok or non-stick frying-pan with 2 tablespoons of stock for 1 minute. Add remaining stock, wine or sherry, bean curd and pepper. Cover and simmer for 3 minutes. Stir in cornflour mix and simmer and stir for 1 minute. Serve hot, garnished with fresh coriander.

CONGHUA GREEN BEANS IN CHINESE WINE SAUCE

The Conghua Hot Springs north east of Guangzhou (Canton) is a popular holiday destination. When I was there I was lucky enough to stay at a famous old hotel favoured by Mao Tse Tung for his 'rests from the revolution'.

Imperial (Metric)	**American**
1 lb (455g) fresh green beans, trimmed	*1 pound fresh green beans, trimmed*
Sauce:	***Sauce:***
1 tablespoon fresh orange juice	*1 tablespoon fresh orange juice*
2 teaspoons cornflour	*2 teaspoons cornflour*
2 teaspoons low-salt soy sauce	*2 teaspoons low-salt soy sauce*
3 tablespoons Chinese wine or dry sherry	*3 tablespoons Chinese wine or dry sherry*

Steam beans vigorously in a steamer for 3 minutes. Remove from heat. Keep warm. To make sauce combine cornflour with orange juice. Add remaining sauce ingredients and bring to the boil stirring continuously. Reduce heat. Simmer for 1 minute, and then pour over beans.

SESAME BEAN CURD

Imperial (Metric)	American
8 fl oz (240ml) basic Chinese vegetable stock	1 cup basic Chinese vegetable stock
1 lb (455g) fresh bean curd, cubed	2 cups fresh bean curd, cubed
8 shallots, sliced	8 shallots, sliced
1 clove garlic, chopped	1 clove garlic, chopped
1 tablespoon low-salt soy sauce	1 tablespoon low-salt soy sauce
2 teaspoons cornflour mixed with 1 tablespoon cold water	2 teaspoons cornflour mixed with 1 tablespoon cold water
2 tablespoons toasted sesame seeds	2 tablespoons toasted sesame seeds

Bring stock to the boil. Add all ingredients except
cornflour and sesame seeds and simmer for 5 minutes.
Stir in cornflour mixture. Simmer for 2 minutes.
Sprinkle with sesame seeds and serve.

Mum's Bean Curd with Fresh
Coriander Sauce (page 75).

Steamed Aubergine (Eggplant) with Hot Garlic Sauce (page 77).

Peppers in Black Bean Sauce
(page 94).

The Canton Crunch (page 99).

CABBAGE IN CREAM SAUCE

Imperial (Metric)	American
1 lb (455g) Chinese cabbage, roughly chopped	1 pound (4 cups) Chinese cabbage, roughly chopped
8 fl oz (240ml) basic Chinese vegetable stock	1 cup basic Chinese vegetable stock
4 fl oz (120ml) skimmed milk	½ cup skim milk
1 tablespoon cornflour	1 tablespoon cornflour
Freshly ground pepper	Freshly ground pepper

Braise cabbage in a pan with ½ cup vegetable stock for 5 minutes. Remove cabbage from pan. Transfer to deep serving bowl and keep warm.

In a saucepan mix remaining vegetable stock, milk and cornflour. Heat gently until the sauce thickens. Season with pepper and pour over cabbage. Serve hot.

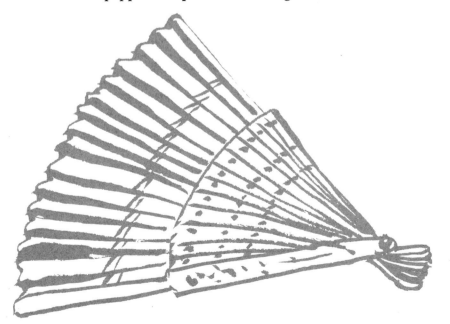

STEAMED MIXED VEGETABLES

Imperial (Metric)
1½ lb (680g) diced mixed vegetables (broccoli, mangetout, shallots, cabbage, celery, green pepper)
1 tablespoon ginger, finely chopped
2 tablespoons Chinese wine or dry sherry
1 tablespoon low-salt soy sauce
Freshly ground pepper

American
4 cups diced mixed vegetables (broccoli, snow peas, shallots, cabbage, celery, green pepper)
1 tablespoon ginger, finely chopped
2 tablespoons Chinese wine or dry sherry
1 tablespoon low-salt soy sauce
Freshly ground pepper

Mix all ingredients together and place in a shallow heatproof bowl. Transfer to steamer and steam vigorously for 15 minutes — until vegetables are tender.

Serve hot.

WHITE COOKED SPINACH WITH SWEET AND SOUR SAUCE

Imperial (Metric)	**American**
12 fl oz (340ml) basic Chinese vegetable stock	1½ cups basic Chinese vegetable stock
1 bunch of spinach, roughly chopped	1 bunch of spinach, roughly chopped
Sauce:	***Sauce:***
2 teaspoons vinegar	2 teaspoons vinegar
4 tablespoons fresh orange juice	4 tablespoons fresh orange juice
2 tablespoons unsweetened tomato juice	2 tablespoons unsweetened tomato juice
2 tablespoons Chinese wine or dry sherry	2 tablespoons Chinese wine or dry sherry
1 tablespoon cornflour	1 tablespoon cornflour

Bring stock to the boil. Add spinach, cover and simmer for 10 minutes. Transfer spinach to dish. Reserve stock. Mix sauce ingredients and bring to the boil. Add reserved stock. Reduce heat and simmer and stir for 2 minutes until sauce thickens.

Spoon sauce over spinach.

TOMATOES IN CREAM SAUCE

Imperial (Metric)	American
1 lb (455g) tomatoes	6–8 medium-sized tomatoes
2 tablespoons water	2 tablespoons water
1 tablespoon Chinese wine or sherry	1 tablespoon Chinese wine or sherry
8 fl oz (240ml) skimmed milk	1 cup skim milk
2 teaspoons cornflour	2 teaspoons cornflour

Blanch tomatoes in a pot of boiling water for 30 seconds. Drain, peel and cut into quarters. Simmer tomatoes in a wok or non-stick frying-pan with 2 tablespoons of water for 5 minutes. Mix wine or sherry with milk and cornflour. Add to wok and simmer until mixture thickens.

Serve hot.

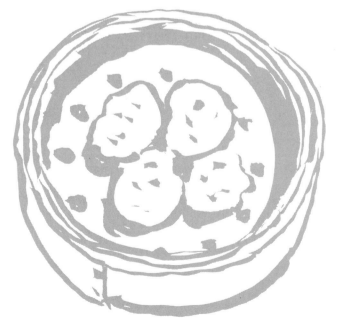

STIR FRIED LETTUCE

Imperial (Metric)	American
1 large lettuce, roughly chopped	1 large lettuce, roughly chopped
1 tablespoon fresh ginger, finely chopped	1 tablespoon finely chopped fresh ginger
1 clove garlic, finely chopped	1 clove garlic, finely chopped
3 tablespoons basic Chinese vegetable stock	3 tablespoons basic Chinese vegetable stock
1 teaspoon cornflour	1 teaspoon cornflour
2 tablespoons Chinese wine or dry sherry	2 tablespoons Chinese wine or dry sherry
1 tablespoon low-salt soy sauce	1 tablespoon low-salt soy sauce

Stir fry lettuce, ginger and garlic in half the stock for 2 minutes over high heat.

Mix cornflour, wine or sherry, soy sauce and remaining stock. Add to frying-pan. Bring to the boil and simmer for 1 minute. Serve hot.

RED COOKED CABBAGE

Imperial (Metric)	**American**
1 Chinese cabbage, roughly chopped	1 Chinese cabbage, roughly chopped
1 tablespoon fresh ginger, finely chopped	1 tablespoon finely chopped fresh ginger
2 cloves garlic, finely chopped	2 cloves garlic, finely chopped
2 shallots, finely chopped	2 shallots, finely chopped
1 red chilli, finely chopped	1 red chili, finely chopped
12 fl oz (340ml) basic Chinese vegetable stock	1½ cups basic Chinese vegetable stock
2 tablespoons low-salt soy sauce	2 tablespoons low-salt soy sauce
1 tablespoon fresh orange juice	1 tablespoon fresh orange juice

Stir fry cabbage, ginger, garlic, shallots and chilli in half the stock for 3 minutes. Reduce heat. Add remaining stock, soy sauce and orange juice. Simmer for another 5 minutes and serve.

STIR FRIED BROCCOLI WITH BAMBOO SHOOTS AND WATER CHESTNUTS

Imperial (Metric)	American
½ lb (225g) broccoli, roughly chopped	2 cups broccoli, roughly chopped
2 tablespoons bean sprouts	2 tablespoons bean sprouts
2 cloves garlic, finely chopped	2 cloves garlic, finely chopped
2 teaspoons fresh ginger, finely chopped	2 teaspoons finely chopped fresh ginger
4 tablespoons water chestnuts, thinly sliced	½ cup water chestnuts, thinly sliced
5 tablespoons basic Chinese vegetable stock	5 tablespoons basic Chinese vegetable stock
2 tablespoons bamboo shoots, thinly sliced	2 tablespoons bamboo shoots, thinly sliced
1 tablespoon low-salt soy sauce	1 tablespoon low-salt soy sauce
2 tablespoons Chinese wine or dry sherry	2 tablespoons Chinese wine or dry sherry
1 teaspoon cornflour	1 teaspoon cornflour

Stir fry broccoli, bean sprouts, garlic and ginger in a non-stick frying-pan for 3 minutes with 3 tablespoons of stock. Add water chestnuts and bamboo shoots and toss for 1 minute.

Mix soy sauce, Chinese wine or sherry with cornflour and remaining vegetable stock. Add to frying-pan. Simmer for 1 minute and serve.

STIR FRIED SPINACH AND BAMBOO SHOOTS

Imperial (Metric)

1 lb (455g) spinach, roughly chopped

2 tablespoons tinned bamboo shoots, thinly sliced

2 teaspoons fresh ginger, finely chopped

1 clove garlic, finely chopped

3 tablespoons basic Chinese vegetable stock

2 tablespoons Chinese wine or dry sherry

1 tablespoon low-salt soy sauce

1 teaspoon cornflour

American

1 pound spinach, roughly chopped

2 tablespoons canned bamboo shoots, thinly sliced

2 teaspoons finely chopped fresh ginger

1 clove garlic, finely chopped

3 tablespoons basic Chinese vegetable stock

2 tablespoons Chinese wine or dry sherry

1 tablespoon low-salt soy sauce

1 teaspoon cornflour

Add spinach, bamboo shoots, ginger, and garlic to wok or non-stick frying-pan. Stir fry for 2 minutes with 3 tablespoons of stock.

Mix sherry, soy sauce and cornflour. Add to wok and simmer until sauce thickens — about 1 minute. Serve hot.

BRAISED MIXED VEGETABLES

Imperial (Metric)	American
4 oz (115g) mangetout, stems and strings removed	1 cup snow peas, stems and strings removed
5 oz (140g) Chinese cabbage, roughly chopped	1¼ cups Chinese cabbage, roughly chopped
6 dried Chinese mushrooms (Soaked in hot water for 30 minutes. Discard stems and cut into quarters.)	6 dried Chinese mushrooms (Soaked in hot water for 30 minutes. Discard stems and cut into quarters.)
1 medium carrot, cut into thin slices	1 medium carrot, cut into thin slices
1 small red or green pepper, seeded and cut into strips	1 small red or green pepper, seeded and cut into strips
8 fl oz (240ml) basic Chinese vegetable stock	1 cup basic Chinese vegetable stock
3½ oz (100g) bean sprouts	1¾ cups bean sprouts
2 shallots, finely diced	2 shallots, finely diced
1 tablespoon low-salt soy sauce	1 tablespoon low-salt soy sauce
2 tablespoons Chinese wine or dry sherry	2 tablespoons Chinese wine or dry sherry
1 teaspoon cornflour	1 teaspoon cornflour
1 tablespoon toasted sesame seeds	1 tablespoon toasted sesame seeds
Freshly ground pepper	Freshly ground pepper

Stir fry mangetout (snow peas), cabbage, mushrooms, carrots and pepper strips in a non-stick frying-pan with half the vegetable stock for 2 minutes. Add bean sprouts and shallots. Toss for 30 seconds. Mix soy sauce, wine or sherry and remaining stock with cornflour. Add to frying-pan and simmer for 2 minutes. Sprinkle with sesame seeds. Season with pepper and serve.

STEAMED BROCCOLI AND CAULIFLOWER

Imperial (Metric)	**American**
8 oz (225g) broccoli florets	*2 cups broccoli flowerets*
8 oz (225g) cauliflower, roughly chopped	*2 cups cauliflower, roughly chopped*
1 tablespoon low-salt soy sauce	*1 tablespoon low-salt soy sauce*
1 tablespoon Chinese wine or dry sherry	*1 tablespoon Chinese wine or dry sherry*
2 tablespoons Basic Chinese Vegetable Stock	*2 tablespoons Basic Chinese Vegetable Stock*
2 teaspoons fresh ginger, finely chopped	*2 teaspoons finely chopped fresh ginger*
3 dried Chinese mushrooms (Soaked in hot water for 30 minutes. Discard stems and cut into quarters.)	*3 dried Chinese mushrooms (Soaked in hot water for 30 minutes. Discard stems and cut into quarters.)*
1 shallot, finely chopped	*1 shallot, finely chopped*

Marinate broccoli and cauliflower with soy sauce, wine or sherry, stock and ginger for 15 minutes. Place marinated vegetables in a heatproof dish with mushrooms on top. Steam vigorously for 20 minutes. Garnish with shallots and serve.

STIR FRIED BEAN SPROUTS

Imperial (Metric)	**American**
1 lb (455g) bean sprouts	1 pound (8 cups) bean sprouts
2 shallots, finely chopped	2 shallots, finely chopped
2 cloves garlic, finely chopped	2 cloves garlic, finely chopped
3 tablespoons basic Chinese vegetable stock	3 tablespoons basic Chinese vegetable stock
Freshly ground pepper	Freshly ground pepper
Sauce:	**Sauce:**
2 tablespoons Chinese wine or dry sherry	2 tablespoons Chinese wine or dry sherry
1 tablespoon low-salt soy sauce	1 tablespoon low-salt soy sauce
1 tablespoon basic Chinese vegetable stock	1 tablespoon basic Chinese vegetable stock
1 teaspoon cornflour	1 teaspoon cornflour

Stir fry bean sprouts, shallots and garlic in a non-stick frying-pan for 2 minutes with 3 tablespoons of vegetable stock.

Mix sauce ingredients. Add to frying-pan and simmer for 1 minute. Season with pepper and serve.

FRESH BEAN CURD WITH SWEET AND SOUR SAUCE

Imperial (Metric)	American
8 oz (225g) fresh bean curd, cubed	1 cup fresh bean curd, cubed
1¼ pints (710ml) water	3 cups water

Sauce:	**Sauce:**
2 teaspoons vinegar	2 teaspoons vinegar
4 tablespoons fresh orange juice	4 tablespoons fresh orange juice
2 tablespoons unsweetened tomato juice	2 tablespoons unsweetened tomato juice
2 tablespoons Chinese wine or dry sherry	2 tablespoons Chinese wine or dry sherry
1 tablespoon water	1 tablespoon water
1 tablespoon cornflour	1 tablespoon cornflour

Rinse bean curd and drain. Bring water to the boil and simmer bean curd for 4 minutes. Remove from water and drain.

Mix sauce ingredients and bring to the boil in saucepan. Reduce heat and simmer for 2 minutes. Add bean curd and simmer for a further 2 minutes. Gently stir to prevent breaking up bean curd.

Serve hot.

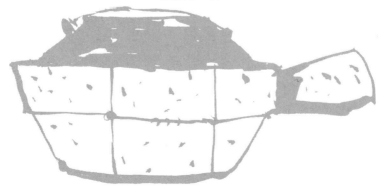

STIR FRIED GREEN PEPPERS AND CHINESE MUSHROOMS

Imperial (Metric)

6 Chinese mushrooms (Soaked in hot water for 30 minutes. Remove stems and cut them into quarters.)

3 cloves garlic, chopped

3 large green peppers, diced

3 tablespoons basic Chinese vegetable stock

2 tablespoons Chinese wine or dry sherry

1 tablespoon low-salt soy sauce

1 teaspoon cornflour

Freshly ground pepper

American

6 Chinese mushrooms (Soaked in hot water for 30 minutes. Remove stems and cut them into quarters.)

3 cloves garlic, chopped

3 large green peppers, diced

3 tablespoons basic Chinese vegetable stock

2 tablespoons Chinese wine or dry sherry

1 tablespoon low-salt soy sauce

1 teaspoon cornflour

Freshly ground pepper

Stir fry mushrooms, garlic and green peppers with stock in non-stick frying-pan for 3 minutes. Mix wine or sherry, soy sauce and cornflour. Add to frying-pan and simmer for 2 minutes. Season with pepper. Serve hot.

GREEN PEPPERS AND CUCUMBER IN BLACK BEAN SAUCE

Imperial (Metric)	American
3 garlic cloves, finely chopped	3 garlic cloves, finely chopped
1 tablespoon black beans (Soaked in cold water for 15 minutes to remove excess salt. Drain and mash.)	1 tablespoon black beans (Soaked in cold water for 15 minutes to remove excess salt. Drain and mash.)
1 red chilli, finely chopped	1 red chili, finely chopped
1 shallot, finely chopped	1 shallot, finely chopped
5 tablespoons basic Chinese vegetable stock	5 tablespoons basic Chinese vegetable stock
3 medium green peppers, seeded and cut into strips	3 medium green peppers, seeded and cut into strips
1 medium cucumber, cut into strips	1 medium cucumber, cut into strips
2 tablespoons Chinese wine or dry sherry	2 tablespoons Chinese wine or dry sherry
1 teaspoon cornflour	1 teaspoon cornflour
Freshly ground pepper	Freshly ground pepper

Add garlic, black beans, chilli and shallots to non-stick frying-pan. Stir fry for 2 minutes with 3 tablespoons of stock. Add green peppers and cucumber to frying-pan and stir fry for 3 minutes.

Mix sherry, cornflour and remaining vegetable stock. Add to frying-pan. Simmer for 1 minute. Season with pepper and serve.

STIR FRIED COURGETTES (ZUCCHINI)

Imperial (Metric)	American
1 lb (455g) courgettes, cut into thin slices	1 pound (2⅔ cups) zucchini, cut into thin slices
2 cloves garlic, finely chopped	2 cloves garlic, finely chopped
2 teaspoons fresh ginger, finely chopped	2 teaspoons finely chopped fresh ginger
1 shallot, finely chopped	1 shallot, fincly chopped
3 tablespoons basic Chinese vegetable stock	3 tablespoons basic Chinese vegetable stock
2 tablespoons Chinese wine or dry sherry	2 tablespoons Chinese wine or dry sherry
1 tablespoon low-salt soy sauce	1 tablespoon low-salt soy sauce
1 teaspoon cornflour	1 teaspoon cornflour
Freshly ground pepper	Freshly ground pepper

Stir fry courgettes (zucchini), garlic, ginger and shallot in non-stick frying-pan with the vegetable stock for 3 minutes.

Mix wine or sherry, soy sauce and cornflour. Add to frying-pan. Simmer for 2 minutes. Season with pepper and serve.

CHINESE SALADS

Yes, the Chinese do eat salads! They are superb served on their own or with a selection of dishes for a Chinese meal or banquet.

BEAN CURD SALAD

Imperial (Metric)	American
1 lb (455g) fresh bean curd, steamed for 3 minutes and diced	2 cups fresh bean curd, steamed for 3 minutes and diced
1 teaspoon fresh ginger, finely chopped	1 teaspoon finely chopped fresh ginger
1 tablespoon low-salt soy sauce	1 tablespoon low-salt soy sauce
1 tablespoon vinegar	1 tablespoon vinegar
1 tablespoon toasted sesame seeds	1 tablespoon toasted sesame seeds

Combine all ingredients. Marinate for 30 minutes and serve.

THE CANTON CRUNCH

A fresh sprout combination.

Imperial (Metric)	American
8 oz (225g) mixed sprouts — bean, alfalfa, mung	4 cups mixed sprouts — bean, alfalfa, mung
3 shallots, diced	3 shallots, diced
2 carrots, grated	2 carrots, grated
8 oz (225g) red cabbage, finely shredded	2 cups red cabbage, finely shredded
8 fl oz (240ml) basic Chinese vegetable stock	1 cup basic Chinese vegetable stock
1 teaspoon fresh ginger, chopped	1 teaspoon chopped fresh ginger
2 cloves garlic, chopped	2 cloves garlic, chopped
1 tablespoon toasted sesame seeds	1 tablespoon toasted sesame seeds
1 tablespoon low-salt soy sauce	1 tablespoon low-salt soy sauce
Freshly ground pepper	Freshly ground pepper
2 tablespoons fresh lemon juice	2 tablespoons fresh lemon juice

Toss and stir all ingredients together except lemon juice. Sprinkle with lemon juice just before serving.

BEIJING AUBERGINE
(EGGPLANT) SALAD

Imperial (Metric)	American
2 medium aubergines	2 medium eggplants
7 fl oz (200ml) basic Chinese vegetable stock or water	¾ cup basic Chinese vegetable stock or water
2 cloves garlic, chopped	2 cloves garlic, chopped
1 teaspoon fresh ginger, finely chopped	1 teaspoon finely chopped fresh ginger
1 tablespoon fresh coriander leaves, chopped	1 tablespoon chopped fresh coriander

Cut aubergine (eggplants) in half lengthwise, then into thin strips. Bring stock to the boil and stir fry aubergine (eggplant) strips with garlic and ginger for 2 minutes. Drain and allow to cool. Garnish with fresh coriander and serve.

SUMMER PALACE CARROT SALAD

The Summer Palace in Beijing (Peking) was originally
built in the twelfth century and, although it has been
extensively rebuilt, the architecture and gardens are
breathtaking. When I was there I also visited the Hall
of Benevolence and Longevity — maybe that's where
the inspiration for this book was founded.

Imperial (Metric)	American
1½ lb (680g) grated carrot	4 cups grated carrot
1 oz (30g) fresh coriander leaves, chopped	1 cup chopped fresh coriander
3 oz (85g) shallots, sliced	½ cup shallots, sliced
1 teaspoon vinegar	1 teaspoon vinegar
1 fresh red chilli, chopped	1 fresh red chili, chopped
1 tablespoon toasted sesame seeds	1 tablespoon toasted sesame seeds
6 fl oz (170ml) fresh orange juice	¾ cup fresh orange juice
½ oz fresh bean sprouts	¼ cup fresh bean sprouts

Combine all ingredients. Marinate for 30 minutes
before serving.

CANTONESE PICKLED VEGETABLES

This delicious sweet and sour dish is made using fresh ingredients, and is a great accompaniment to any Chinese meal.

Imperial (Metric)	**American**
1 cucumber, thinly sliced	1 cucumber, thinly sliced
2 carrots, cut into thin strips	2 carrots, cut into thin strips
4 oz (115g) cauliflower florets	1 cup cauliflower flowerets
3 sticks celery, diced	3 sticks celery, diced
1 clove garlic, chopped	1 clove garlic, chopped
½ teaspoon fresh ginger, finely chopped	½ teaspoon finely chopped fresh ginger
8 fl oz (240ml) fresh orange juice	1 cup fresh orange juice
1 tablespoon vinegar	1 tablespoon vinegar
Freshly ground pepper	Freshly ground pepper

Place cucumber, carrots, cauliflower and celery in a serving bowl. Mix together remaining ingredients and pour over vegetables. Combine well and marinate for 1 hour before serving.

YUM YUM RAW CHINESE SALAD

Imperial (Metric)

1 lb (455g) Chinese cabbage, shredded

6 oz (170g) water chestnuts, diced

1 small white onion, finely chopped

2 shallots, sliced

¾ lb (340g) carrot, grated

4 oz (115g) bean sprouts

1 tablespoon toasted sesame seeds

8 fl oz (240ml) fresh orange juice

1 tablespoon low-salt soy sauce

American

4 cups shredded Chinese cabbage

1 cup diced water chestnuts

1 small white onion, finely chopped

2 shallots, sliced

2 cups carrot, grated

2 cups bean sprouts

1 tablespoon toasted sesame seeds

1 cup fresh orange juice

1 tablespoon low-salt soy sauce

Combine all ingredients and serve.

COLD NOODLE SALAD

Imperial (Metric)	**American**
2 lb (900g) cooked wholewheat or rice noodles	5 cups cooked wholewheat or rice noodles
6 oz (170g) carrot, grated	1 cup carrot, grated
1½ oz (45g) shallots, diced	¼ cup diced shallots
2 oz (55g) red cabbage, finely shredded	½ cup finely shredded red cabbage
1 clove garlic, chopped	1 clove garlic, chopped
1 teaspoon fresh ginger, finely chopped	1 teaspoon finely chopped fresh ginger
1 tablespoon low-salt soy sauce	1 tablespoon low-salt soy sauce
4 tablespoons fresh lemon juice	¼ cup fresh lemon juice
2 teaspoons toasted sesame seeds	2 teaspoons toasted sesame seeds

Combine all ingredients and serve.

CUCUMBER SALAD

Imperial (Metric)	American
3 medium cucumbers	3 medium cucumbers
1 clove garlic, chopped	1 clove garlic, chopped
1 teaspoon fresh ginger, finely chopped	1 teaspoon finely chopped fresh ginger
1 teaspoon vinegar	1 teaspoon vinegar
1 tablespoon low-salt soy sauce	1 tablespoon low-salt soy sauce
4 fl oz (120ml) fresh orange juice	½ cup fresh orange juice
1 teaspoon freshly ground Szechuan or black pepper	1 teaspoon freshly ground Szechuan or black pepper
1 tablespoon toasted sesame seeds	1 tablespoon toasted sesame seeds

Peel cucumbers and slice into thin discs. Mix with other ingredients except sesame seeds. Marinate for 30 minutes before serving. Toss in sesame seeds and serve.

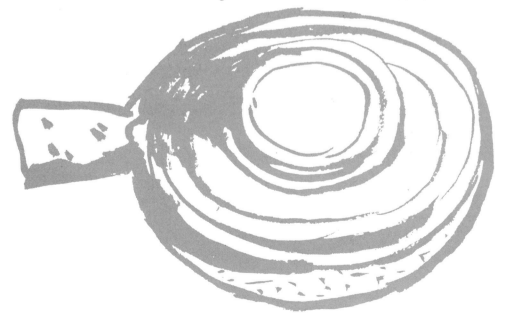

RICE &
NOODLES

HOW TO COOK BROWN RICE

Absorption Method
Use the following guidelines for cooking 'perfect' rice every time.

1 cup rice   — 2 cups water
2 cups rice — 3½ cups water
3 cups rice — 5 cups water

Firstly wash rice in cold water and drain in a colander. Bring rice and water to the boil in a large saucepan. Turn heat to very low. Cover saucepan with tight-fitting lid and cook for 35–40 minutes. Do not lift lid during cooking process. Remove from heat, uncover, and fluff rice with a fork for a few minutes.

RICE CONGEE

This thick rice soup is called *jook*. In Southern China it
was often served to us at breakfast time. It is
nourishing and flavoursome, and certainly gave me the
'pedal power' I needed for my bicycle tour of China.

Imperial (Metric)

3½ pints (2 litres) basic Chinese
vegetable stock

8 oz (225g) brown rice

6 oz (170g) shallots, finely chopped

6 oz (170g) water chestnuts,
chopped

3 oz (85g) grated carrot

1 oz (30g) bean sprouts

2 teaspoons fresh ginger, finely
chopped

8 fl oz (240ml) skimmed milk

2 teaspoons low-salt soy sauce

Garnish:
Sprinkling of toasted sesame seeds

American

8 cups basic Chinese vegetable
stock

2 cups brown rice

1 cup shallots, finely chopped

1 cup water chestnuts, chopped

½ cup grated carrot

½ cup bean sprouts

2 teaspoons finely chopped fresh
ginger

1 cup skim milk

2 teaspoons low-salt soy sauce

Garnish:
Sprinkling of toasted sesame seeds

Bring stock to the boil. Add rice. Reduce heat, cover
and simmer for 2½ hours. The congee should be thick
and glutinous. Add remaining ingredients except
garnish and simmer for 15 minutes. Garnish and serve.

SINGAPORE CHINESE NOODLES

Imperial (Metric)	American
14 oz (395g) fresh rice noodles, cut into thin strips	*2½ cups fresh rice noodles, cut into thin strips*
7 oz (200g) bean curd, diced	*1 cup bean curd, diced*
4 oz (115g) bean sprouts	*2 cups bean sprouts*
6 oz (170g) shallots, sliced	*1 cup sliced shallots*
8 dried Chinese mushrooms (Soaked for 30 minutes in hot water. Discard stems and finely slice.)	*8 dried Chinese mushrooms (Soaked for 30 minutes in hot water. Discard stems and finely slice.)*
2 fresh red chillies, chopped	*2 fresh red chillis, chopped*
1 green pepper, finely sliced	*1 green pepper, finely sliced*
1 red pepper, finely sliced	*1 red pepper, finely sliced*
5 tablespoons basic Chinese vegetable stock	*5 tablespoons basic Chinese vegetable stock*
Sauce:	***Sauce:***
2 cloves garlic, chopped	*2 cloves garlic, chopped*
2 teaspoons fresh ginger, chopped	*2 teaspoons chopped fresh ginger*
1 tablespoon low-salt soy sauce	*1 tablespoon low-salt soy sauce*
1 tablespoon Chinese wine or dry sherry	*1 tablespoon Chinese wine or dry sherry*
2 teaspoons sesame seeds	*2 teaspoons sesame seeds*
1 teaspoon cornflour	*1 teaspoon cornflour*
1 teaspoon fresh orange juice	*1 teaspoon fresh orange juice*
Freshly ground pepper	*Freshly ground pepper*
3 tablespoons basic Chinese vegetable stock	*3 tablespoons basic Chinese vegetable stock*
1 tablespoon mild/medium hot curry powder	*1 tablespoon mild/medium hot curry powder*

Mix sauce ingredients in a bowl. Bring a large saucepan of water to the boil. Plunge in noodles for 30

110

seconds. Remove and drain. Stir fry bean curd in a hot wok or non-stick frying-pan for 1 minute with 2 tablespoons of vegetable stock. Remove bean curd from wok and set aside. Stir fry bean sprouts, shallots, mushrooms, peppers, and chillies for 2 minutes in wok with 3 tablespoons of vegetable stock. Return bean curd and noodles to wok. Add sauce and toss over low heat for 2 minutes. Serve hot.

VEGETABLE FRIED RICE

Imperial (Metric)	**American**
3 cloves garlic, finely chopped	3 cloves garlic, finely chopped
1 tablespoon ginger, finely chopped	1 tablespoon ginger, finely chopped
3 shallots, chopped	3 shallots, chopped
3 tablespoons basic Chinese vegetable stock	3 tablespoons basic Chinese vegetable stock
1 green pepper, deseeded and cut into strips	1 green pepper, seeded and cut into strips
4 oz (115g) broccoli, chopped	1 cup broccoli, chopped
2 oz (55g) bean sprouts	1 cup bean sprouts
1 tablespoon low-salt soy sauce	1 tablespoon low-salt soy sauce
2 tablespoons Chinese wine or dry sherry	2 tablespoons Chinese wine or dry sherry
1 lb 2 oz (510g) cooked brown rice	3 cups cooked brown rice
Freshly ground pepper	Freshly ground pepper

Stir fry garlic, ginger and shallots in non-stick frying-pan for 1 minute with 1 tablespoon of stock.

Add green pepper, broccoli and bean sprouts to frying-pan and stir fry for 3 minutes with 2 tablespoons of stock.

Sprinkle soy sauce and Chinese wine or sherry into frying-pan. Add rice to pan and stir fry over medium heat until heated through. Season with pepper and serve hot. If you like spicy fried rice, add a diced red or green chilli.

Singapore Chinese Noodles (page 110).

Lychee and Ginger Ice Cream (page 122).

Steamed Wholemeal Date Buns
(page 124).

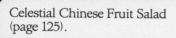

Celestial Chinese Fruit Salad
(page 125).

COMBINATION CHOW MEIN

Imperial (Metric)	American
1 lb (455g) fresh rice noodles	3 cups fresh rice noodles
4 tablespoons basic Chinese vegetable stock	4 tablespoons basic Chinese vegetable stock
2 oz (55g) bean sprouts	1 cup bean sprouts
4 oz (115g) broccoli florets	1 cup broccoli flowerets
8 mangetout, ends trimmed	8 snow peas, trimmed
6 oz (170g) bamboo shoots	1 cup bamboo shoots
2 cloves garlic, sliced	2 cloves garlic, chopped
6 oz (170g) carrots, sliced	1 cup sliced carrots
5 dried Chinese mushrooms (Soaked in hot water for 30 minutes. Discard stems and slice.)	5 dried Chinese mushrooms (Soaked in hot water for 30 minutes. Discard stems and slice.)

Sauce:	*Sauce:*
2 teaspoons cornflour	2 teaspoons cornflour
1 tablespoon Chinese wine or dry sherry	1 tablespoon Chinese wine or dry sherry
4 fl oz (120ml) Chinese vegetable stock	½ cup basic Chinese vegetable stock
1 tablespoon low-salt soy sauce	1 tablespoon low-salt soy sauce
1 tablespoon diced shallots	1 tablespoon diced shallots
Freshly ground pepper	Freshly ground pepper
1 teaspoon fresh ginger, chopped	1 teaspoon chopped fresh ginger

Drop noodles into boiling water. Reduce heat. Simmer
for 1 minute and drain. Stir fry remaining ingredients
in a non-stick frying-pan or wok for 3 minutes with 4
tablespoons of stock.

Return drained noodles to frying-pan.

Mix sauce ingredients. Pour sauce over chow mein and
toss for 3 minutes over low heat. Serve hot.

STIR FRIED RICE NOODLES AND GREEN PEPPERS WITH BLACK BEAN SAUCE

Imperial (Metric)	American
3 cloves garlic, finely chopped	3 cloves garlic, finely chopped
1 tablespoon black beans (Soaked in cold water for 15 minutes to remove excess salt. Drain and mash.)	1 tablespoon black beans (Soaked in cold water for 15 minutes to remove excess salt. Drain and mash.)
2 shallots, finely chopped	2 shallots, finely chopped
2 teaspoons fresh ginger, finely chopped	2 teaspoons finely chopped fresh ginger
2 medium green peppers, deseeded and cut into strips	2 medium green peppers, seeded and cut into strips
3 tablespoons basic Chinese vegetable stock	3 tablespoons basic Chinese vegetable stock
1 lb (455g) fresh rice noodles, cut into strips	3 cups fresh rice noodles, cut into strips
2 tablespoons Chinese wine or dry sherry	2 tablespoons Chinese wine or dry sherry
2 tablespoons basic Chinese vegetable stock	2 tablespoons basic Chinese vegetable stock
2 teaspoons cornflour	2 teaspoons cornflour

Stir fry garlic, black beans, shallots, ginger and green peppers in a non-stick frying-pan with 3 tablespoons of stock for 3 minutes.

Bring a large saucepan of water to the boil. Plunge rice noodles in for 1 minute. Remove and drain.

Mix two tablespoons vegetable stock, Chinese wine or sherry and cornflour. Add to frying-pan. Add rice noodles and stir over low for heat for 2 minutes. Serve hot.

STIR FRIED RICE NOODLES WITH LETTUCE AND MUSHROOMS

Imperial (Metric)	American
1 small lettuce, roughly chopped	1 small lettuce roughly chopped
6 dried Chinese mushrooms (Soaked in hot water for 30 minutes. Discard stems and cut into quarters.)	6 dried Chinese mushrooms (Soaked in hot water for 30 minutes. Discard stems and cut into quarters.)
2 cloves garlic, finely chopped	2 cloves garlic, finely chopped
1 tablespoon fresh ginger, finely chopped	1 tablespoon finely chopped fresh ginger
1 shallot, finely chopped	1 shallot, finely chopped
8 fl oz (240ml) basic Chinese vegetable stock	1 cup basic Chinese vegetable stock
1 lb (455g) fresh rice noodles, cut into strips	3 cups fresh rice noodles, cut into strips
1 tablespoon low-salt soy sauce	1 tablespoon low-salt soy sauce
2 tablespoons Chinese wine or dry sherry	2 tablespoons Chinese wine or dry sherry
2 teaspoons cornflour	2 teaspoons cornflour
Freshly ground pepper	Freshly ground pepper

Stir fry lettuce, mushrooms, garlic, ginger, and shallots with half the stock in a non-stick frying-pan for 3 minutes. Bring a large saucepan of water to the boil. Plunge in noodles for 1 minute. Remove and drain.

Mix soy sauce, wine or sherry and cornflour with remaining stock and add to frying-pan. Stir in rice noodles. Season with pepper and simmer for 2 minutes.

Serve hot.

DESSERTS

The Chinese enjoy desserts, and the emphasis is usually on seasonal fruits.

In Western Chinese restaurants the dish lychees and ice cream is popular.

In China I was served delicious steamed buns stuffed with dried fruit — often for breakfast!

MELON BASKET

Imperial (Metric)	American
1 small watermelon	1 small watermelon
1 medium canteloupe melon	1 medium rockmelon (canteloupe)
1 medium honeydew melon	1 medium honeydew melon
8 fl oz (240ml) fresh orange juice	1 cup fresh orange juice
8 fl oz (240ml) sweet sherry	1 cup sweet sherry

Cut the melons in half and scrape out seeds. With a melon baller scoop out balls of fruit. Combine all fruits. Pour over juice and sherry and marinate in refrigerator for 30 minutes before serving. This dessert looks attractive served in hollowed-out watermelon.

Garnish: fresh mint leaves

LYCHEE FRUIT WHIP

Imperial (Metric)	American
12 fl oz (340ml) skimmed milk	1½ cups skim milk
6 oz (170g) fresh or tinned lychees (Remove lychee stones from fresh ones. Rinse tinned lychees to remove excess sugar.)	1 cup fresh or canned lychees (Remove lychee stones from fresh ones. Rinse canned lychees to remove excess sugar.)
8 fl oz (240ml) crushed ice	1 cup crushed ice
1 tablespoon sweet sherry	1 tablespoon sweet sherry

Blend all ingredients until ice is well combined.

STUFFED LYCHEES

Imperial (Metric)	American
6 oz (170g) currants	1 cup currants
2½ oz (70g) toasted sesame seeds	½ cup toasted sesame seeds
6 oz (170g) dried apricots, finely chopped	1 cup finely chopped dried apricots
1 tablespoon sweet sherry	1 tablespoon sweet sherry
20 fresh or tinned lychees (Remove lychee stones from fresh ones. Rinse tinned lychees to remove excess sugar.)	20 fresh or canned lychees (Remove lychee stones from fresh ones. Rinse canned lychees to remove excess sugar.)

Blend together currants, sesame seeds, dried apricots and sherry. Stuff mixture into lychees. Chill and serve.

GINGER PEARS

Imperial (Metric)	American
6 fresh pears, with stems on	6 fresh pears, with stems on
8 fl oz (240ml) unsweetened apple juice	1 cup unsweetened apple juice
8 fl oz (240ml) Chinese wine or dry sherry	1 cup Chinese wine or dry sherry
8 fl oz (240ml) water	1 cup water
Small piece of cinnamon stick	Small piece of cinnamon stick
1 tablespoon fresh ginger, finely chopped	1 tablespoon finely chopped fresh ginger

Combine all ingredients in saucepan. Stand pears upright. Cover and simmer for 20 minutes and serve.

SESAME PEACHES

Imperial (Metric)	American
4 fresh golden peaches	4 fresh golden peaches
5 oz (140g) sesame seeds	1 cup sesame seeds
6 oz (170g) currants	1 cup currants
1 teaspoon cinnamon	1 teaspoon cinnamon
18 fl oz (520ml) Chinese wine or dry sherry	2 cups Chinese wine or dry sherry

Cut peaches in half and remove stones. Blend together sesame seeds, currants and cinnamon. Stuff blended mixture into cavity of peach halves. Place peaches cut side up in non-stick baking dish. Pour over wine or sherry.

Preheat oven to 180°C/375°F (Gas Mark 5). Bake for 25 minutes and serve.

BAKED RICE PUDDING

Imperial (Metric)	American
1½ lb (680g) cooked brown rice	4 cups cooked brown rice
1¾ pints (1 litre) skimmed milk	4 cups skim milk
6 oz (170g) currants	1 cup currants
6 oz (170g) raisins	1 cup raisins
1 teaspoon fresh ginger, finely chopped	1 teaspoon finely chopped fresh ginger
Grated rind of 1 lemon	Grated rind of 1 lemon
1 teaspoon vanilla essence	1 teaspoon vanilla essence
2 egg whites	2 egg whites
2 fl oz (60ml) sweet sherry	¼ cup sweet sherry

Combine all ingredients and place in non-stick baking dish. Preheat oven to 180°C/375°F (Gas Mark 5). Bake for 45 minutes.

LYCHEE AND GINGER ICE CREAM

Imperial (Metric)	American
14 fl oz (400ml) evaporated milk	1¾ cups evaporated milk
4 fl oz (120ml) skimmed milk	½ cup skim milk
½ teaspoon ground ginger	½ teaspoon ground ginger
1 teaspoon vanilla essence	1 teaspoon vanilla essence
1 tablespoon vegetarian gelatine mixed with 2 tablespoons boiling water	1 tablespoon vegetarian gelatine mixed with 2 tablespoons boiling water
1 lb lychees, fresh or tinned, roughly chopped (Remove lychee stones from fresh ones. If using tinned ones, rinse to remove excess sugar.)	3 cups lychees, fresh or canned, roughly chopped (Remove lychee stones from fresh ones. If using canned ones, rinse to remove excess sugar.)
2 teaspoons fresh ginger, finely chopped	2 teaspoons finely chopped fresh ginger
3 egg whites, stiffly beaten	3 egg whites, stiffly beaten

Blend evaporated milk, skimmed milk, ground ginger, vanilla essence and gelatine mixture, until smooth and creamy — about 10 minutes.

Place in freezer for 45 minutes. Blend or beat again for 5 minutes.

Fold in lychees, ginger and stiffly beaten egg whites.

Refreeze.

SESAME CAKE

Imperial (Metric)	American
4 egg whites	4 egg whites
6 oz (170g) self-raising flour	1½ cups self-raising flour
14 oz (395g) sultanas	2 cups sultanas
Rind of 1 orange, grated	Rind of 1 orange, grated
Rind of 1 lemon, grated	Rind of 1 lemon, grated
5 oz (140g) sesame seeds	1 cup sesame seeds
1 teaspoon freshly grated nutmeg	1 teaspoon freshly grated nutmeg

Beat egg whites until stiff. Set aside. Sift flour.
Combine all ingredients and mix thoroughly. Bake in a
non-stick loaf tin in a preheated oven at 200°C/400°F
(Gas Mark 6) for 35 minutes. Allow cake to cool in tin.
Remove, wrap in foil and refrigerate for 24 hours before
cutting.

STEAMED WHOLEMEAL DATE BUNS

Imperial (Metric)	American
4 tablespoons unsweetened apple juice, warmed	4 tablespoons unsweetened apple juice, warmed
½ oz (15g) dried yeast	5 teaspoons dried yeast
1 lb (455g) wholemeal flour	4 cups wholemeal flour
½ teaspoon ground cinnamon	½ teaspoon ground cinnamon
10 fl oz (285ml) warm skimmed milk	1 cup plus 3 tablespoons warm skim milk
2 teaspoons honey (optional)	2 teaspoons honey (optional)
3 oz (85g) fresh or dried stoned dates	½ cup fresh or dried pitted dates

Combine warmed apple juice and dried yeast. Leave in a warm place until it begins to foam.

Sift the flour and cinnamon. Make a well in the centre. Pour in the yeast mixture, skimmed milk and honey (optional). Turn dough onto a floured board and knead until smooth — about 5 minutes. Wrap in plastic and leave in a warm place for 1 hour.

Knead again for 5 minutes, wrap in a clean tea towel and leave for 30 minutes. Knead again for 5 minutes just before you use it. (If dough is too sticky, sprinkle with extra flour.)

Roll out dough and cut into 12 pieces.

Roll each piece into a small ball. Stuff a date into the centre. Squash dough together and twist at the top.

Bring water to the boil and place buns in bamboo or metal steamer. Dab tops of buns with extra unsweetened apple juice. Cover and steam for 15 minutes. Serve hot.

Dates can be substituted with dried apricots.

CELESTIAL CHINESE FRUIT SALAD

Imperial (Metric)	American
5 oz (140g) watermelon balls	1 cup watermelon balls
5 oz (140g) honeydew melon balls	1 cup honeydew melon balls
10 oz (285g) diced fresh pineapple or tinned unsweetened pieces	2 cups diced fresh pineapple or canned unsweetened pieces
5 oz (140g) kiwi fruit, peeled and cut into circles	1 cup kiwi fruit circles
5 oz (140g) diced apple	1 cup diced apple
10 oz (285g) fresh lychees	2 cups fresh lychees
5 oz (140g) sliced fresh mango	1 cup sliced fresh mango
1 tablespoon fresh ginger, finely chopped	1 tablespoon finely chopped fresh ginger
½ clove garlic, crushed (optional)	½ clove crushed garlic (optional)
8 fl oz (240ml) fresh orange juice	1 cup fresh orange juice
8 fl oz (240ml) unsweetened pineapple juice	1 cup unsweetened pineapple juice
Garnish:	*Garnish:*
Fresh rose petals and violets	Fresh rose petals and violets

Combine all ingredients except garnish. Chill before serving and garnish.

Fruit salad can be made with any seasonal fruits.

INDEX

INDEX